# THE
# NATIVITY
## How The Story Of Christmas Can Change Your Life

———————

JAMES COLLINS

On Point Publishing
www.thepointis.net

D1496315

The Nativity
How The Story of Christmas Can Change Your Life
Copyright © 2019 by James Collins
On Point Publishing
www.thepointis.net
*"I will publish the name of the LORD."* **Deuteronomy 32:3**

ISBN 978-0-578-60146-5

All Scripture quotations are from the King James Version of the Holy Bible.

Printed in USA by 48HrBooks (www.48HrBooks.com)
First Printing

# Dedication

To Abbigail, Timothy, and John,
Stay focused on Christ and stay filled with the Spirit of
Christmas.

# Table of Contents

# Acknowledgements

I started my writing ministry with my calendar already full. It has been a crazy and busy adventure that would not have been possible without the support, encouragement, understanding, and selflessness of others.

I am grateful to Dr. Fred Hambrick for his years of mentorship and guidance.

I would like to thank Dr. Larry Baker, Dr. Larry Spargimino, and Brian Foster for their research, friendship, and insights.

Many thanks to my team of editors – Linda VanSickle, Gary VanSickle, and Cindy Foster. Your contributions were spot on. I appreciate you more than you know.

I also want to thank the congregation of First Southern Baptist Church in Fort Scott, Kansas for their patience and support.

Amanda: I love you and feel incredibly blessed to have you in my life. Thank you for allowing me to take the time necessary to write for the Lord.

I thank God for all of you.

James Collins

# Introduction

Once there was a very famous professor of chemistry. The professor patented several industrial chemical compounds and he wrote many books on chemistry. As a result, he became financially well-off and then retired. In his retirement, he became a guest lecturer and speaker at colleges and universities.

As the professor grew older, his eyesight dimmed. His vision problems caused him to have trouble driving. So, the professor hired a chauffeur.

After a year or more, the chauffeur had driven the chemistry professor to dozens of speaking engagements. He had heard the professor give the same speech hundreds of times.

One day, on the way to another speaking engagement, the chauffeur said, "Professor, I have heard you give the same talk a hundred times. I believe I could give your speech myself." The professor said, "I'll bet you $50 you can't." "You're on," said the chauffeur.

The driver stopped the car and the two exchanged clothes. They drove to the college, went into the lecture hall, and sat down. The chauffeur, dressed in the professor's tuxedo, sat at the head table. The dean of the science department stood up and introduced whom he thought was the professor. The chauffeur, who was dressed as the professor, stood up and gave the professor's speech without missing a word. It was perfect – just as if the professor gave it himself.

There was a standing ovation when the chauffeur finished. The dean got up and said, "We are so fortunate to have such a fine resource with us tonight, and since we have a little extra time, let's have some questions and answers." A student stood up in the back and asked, "Professor, the element, strontium when combined with radioactive isotopes does not produce a normal reaction. Why is this?"

The chauffeur stood there with a nervous look on his face. The lecture hall was silent. Everybody was waiting for him to answer. Finally, he said, "That's just about the dumbest question I ever heard. In fact, it is so dumb I bet even my chauffeur could answer that question!"

We can hear something so many times we lose the meaning. How many times have you heard the Christmas story? You probably have heard it hundreds of times. You have heard it so many times, you could stand up and tell it word for word.

Even non-Christians know the story. Ask anyone and they can tell you about Caesar's tax. Everyone knows about Mary and Joseph's trip to Bethlehem. Most people can tell you that Jesus was born in a stable. We've heard it thousands of times.

The story of the birth of Jesus Christ as told in the second chapter of Luke's Gospel is the best-known story in the Bible. The best-known chapter is the 23rd Psalm. The best-known verse is John 3:16. However, Luke Chapter 2, contains the best-known story. The verses in Luke 2 are used over and over in Christmas pageants, plays, cards, TV programs, movies, and music. Sometimes something that is so familiar can lose its impact on our lives. The story of God becoming a man - of God taking on human flesh - can become common for us.

Dr. Jim Rosscup is a professor at the Master's Seminary in Sun Valley, California. Jim was an older man when he got saved. He did not grow up in a Christian family. He knew very little about the Bible when God called him to ministry. When he started at Dallas Theological Seminary, he felt like he was a step behind everyone else. He was very intimidated by the knowledge of his fellow seminary students.

One day, Jim was feeling overwhelmed. He sat down with one of his professors, Dr. Howard Hendricks. Jim said, "Dr. Hendricks, I feel so overwhelmed and so intimidated. It's all so new." Dr. Hendricks looked at him and said, "Let's hope it never becomes old."

That's important for us to remember. Sometimes the greatest truths in the world can become old. Have you heard the story of Christ's birth so often that you think you know it all? My prayer is you will look at these truths in a new way. Over the course of this book, as you study God's Word, I pray that the Christmas Story will be received in a new and fresh way. I pray it will never grow old.

The problem is when something becomes too familiar to us, we have trouble seeing it in a new way. That is the purpose of this book: To help you see beyond the familiar and find the true Spirit of Christmas. It is my prayer that you gain a new appreciation of what God did for us when He broke into history in the person of Jesus Christ.

Each year, after Thanksgiving, our family begins to decorate our home for Christmas. We usually do it on the Friday after Thanksgiving when most people are out shopping. We listen to Christmas music, open the boxes of ornaments and decorations, and with each piece we unpack we are reminded of Christmases past.

Years ago, when my wife, Amanda, and I were dating, we went to a formal military event. Back then, I was a young U.S. Army soldier and my unit was hosting the formal. The event was held in mid-December and each lady received a crystal Christmas tree ornament. The first Christmas after we were married, Amanda hung the ornament on our tree. Each Christmas now, I continue to buy her a special ornament for our tree. It has become a tradition.

When God blessed us with children, they got in on the act. Over the years, the kids have made numerous ornaments. Each ornament has a story and history to it, and our entire family enjoys hanging them on the tree and decorating our house.

A few Christmases after we were married, Amanda came home with our first Nativity set. If you are not familiar with a Nativity set, they are figures or art objects which depict the manger scene of Christ's birth. The other day, I heard someone describe Nativity sets as the Christian alternative to "Elf on a Shelf."

Over the years, we have amassed quite a number. We are always searching flea markets, thrift stores, and garage sales to find a new Nativity to add to our collection.

Most Nativity sets have several different pieces – shepherds, angels, Mary, Joseph, and of course, the Baby Jesus. This book is sort of a living Nativity scene, put together from the Word of God. Each chapter is designed to spotlight a different "figure" from the Nativity. Along the way, you will find timeless, practical, life lessons each person in the Christmas story teaches.

My prayer for you as you read this book is that you would experience the Spirit of Christmas in your life.

# Chapter 1
# THE CRADLE

"The coming of Christ by way of a Bethlehem manger seems strange and stunning. But when we take him out of the manger and invite Him into our hearts, then the meaning unfolds, and the strangeness vanishes."

C. Neil Strait

## The Manger

*"And Jesus said unto him, Foxes have holes, and birds of the air have nests; but the Son of man hath not where to lay his head."*

**Luke 9:58**

The year was 1809. If there had been a CNN or a Fox News, the most prominent story would have been Napoleon and his army tearing through Europe. Napoleon invaded Austria in 1809. It was a bloody and terrible war.

In 1809, Napoleon's invasion of Austria was the focus of the world. No one during this time cared about newborn babies. However, the world overlooked a lot of important births in 1809.

The great poet Alfred Tennyson was born in 1809. Edgar Alan Poe, the famous poet and writer was also born in 1809. Both men had a major impact on literature in the world. Charles Darwin was born in 1809. His theory of evolution has had a tremendous impact on science and faith. Also, in 1809, a baby was born in a log cabin in Kentucky. His name was Abraham Lincoln. He would grow up to be the sixteenth President of the United States. Nevertheless, in 1809, the world was focused on a war in Europe. No one gave any thought to any of these babies born in 1809, and how they would help shape the world.

In the same way, 1800 years earlier, who could have cared about the birth of a baby? The world was watching the Roman Empire. All eyes were on Caesar and the census that he had ordered. Who was interested in a poor couple making the 90-mile journey from Nazareth to Bethlehem? Who cared about the birth of a little Jewish boy? The answer, of course, is God did. A young Jewish woman cradled the biggest news of all time – the birth of our Savior.

The birth of Jesus Christ is the greatest news story of all time. Yet it is a story the world of that day totally missed other than some shepherds and later a few wise men.

The story of the birth of Christ is a story meant to decorate our hearts the way lights decorate a barren Christmas tree. With that in mind, lets look at the story of the nativity.

## THE HISTORICAL BACKGROUND
## OF THE STORY

*"And it came to pass in those days, that there went out a decree from Caesar Augustus that all the world should be taxed."*

**Luke 2:1**

### The Calendar

Luke begins his telling of the birth of Christ with the words, *"And it came to pass in those days."* "Those days" were probably around 4 or 5 BC. The letters BC stand for "before Christ." How could Jesus be born 4 or 5 years before Christ?

The man who developed our calendar was off a little bit. We know Jesus was born before April of 4 BC because that is when Herod died. Obviously, Herod was alive when Jesus was born.

It is easy to lose track of time. The man who developed our calendar lost some time. In the sixth-century, a Roman mathematician and astronomer named Diony-sius Exiguus (Dionysius the Little) reworked the calendar to pinpoint the birth of Christ. He correctly believed the birth of Christ was the midpoint of human history. Unfortunately, his math was off by a few years. The Lord Jesus Christ was born in 4 or 5 BC. The exact year is not as important as a correct understanding of the significance of Jesus' birth.

Many Christians do not believe you should observe Christmas because December 25$^{th}$ was originally a pagan holiday. The fixing of the date of Christmas as December 25$^{th}$ comes from the Roman Emperor Constantine (AD 306–337). The Romans celebrated the Saturnalia festival at the close of December. They also thought December 25$^{th}$ marked the date of the winter solstice and observed the pagan feast of Sol Invictus (the unconquerable sun) on December 25$^{th}$. Constantine changed the day of the worship of the sun to the worship of God's Son. He changed the Roman pagan holiday to a holiday to honor the birth of Jesus Christ.

If Christmas is simply a holiday commandeered from the pagans, does that mean we should not celebrate Christmas? Let's think about that. The pagan traditions have nothing to do with Christ in the Bible. In our day, we do not celebrate the birth of a pagan god, but the Savior of the world. I don't worship a false sun-god on Christmas. I rejoice over the incarnation – the true God becoming flesh.

I fully understand Christmas was in ancient Roman times, a pagan holiday. Anyone would be very hard-pressed to name any day during the year that would not, at some time, have been a pagan holiday. However, today most of the world observes Christmas on December 25th. Christmas is a time in our culture when we are freer to talk about Christ in public settings, sing about Christ, and tell others that He came into the world to save us from our sins. Christmas is a time when the lost are more open to hear the message of Christ.

*"One man esteemeth one day above another: another esteemeth every day alike. Let every man be fully persuaded in his own mind. He that regardeth the day, regardeth it unto the Lord; and he that regardeth not the day, to the Lord he doth not regard it."*

**Romans 14:5-6a**

In Romans Chapter 14, The Apostle Paul wrote about Christian liberty. He said one man may regard a day to the Lord and another man may not regard that day to the Lord. He then concluded the entire section with the strong admonition that we are not to judge one another over such peripheral issues when he said, *"Let us not therefore judge one another any more: but judge this rather, that no man put a stumblingblock or an occasion to fall in his brother's way."*

So, if I want to give spiritual significance to December 25th, I have freedom in Christ to do so, and no other believer has a right to condemn me for doing so.

Nor do I have the right to condemn those who refuse to give any spiritual significance to the day.

Five-year-old Billy was showing his Christmas presents to Grandma when she asked, "Did you get everything you wanted for Christmas?"

Billy thought for a moment before he answered, "No, I didn't, Grandma. But that's okay. It wasn't my birthday."

Billy had the right attitude. It's not about you. It's not about me. It's all about Jesus. It's okay to celebrate His birthday on December 25$^{th}$.

## The Conception

I understand Jesus was not likely born during the month of December. The shepherds did not go into the field with their flocks during the colder months. When Jesus was born, the weather was mild enough for shepherds to be in the fields.

However, there is strong biblical support to prove Jesus was conceived in December. The Bible teaches that life begins at the moment of conception. Therefore, the incarnation began when Christ was conceived by the Holy Spirit in Mary's womb.

In Luke Chapter 1, we read about the conception of John the Baptist. John's father, Zacharias, was a priest of the course of Abia (Luke 1:5). The priesthood was divided into 24 courses because there were so many priests

(1 Chronicles 24). Each order served in the temple one week, twice a year. In other words, they were only in the temple two weeks out of the year. Each time of service was separated by six months.

Zacharias and his wife, Elisabeth, were not only old, they were *"stricken in years"* (Luke 1:7). Being stricken in years, gives the idea that not everything works and everything that does work, hurts. Because of her age, Elisabeth was barren. She was too old to have children.

Zacharias' duty as a priest in the temple was to offer up incense. When the smoke from the incense would rise from the altar, he would pray. As he was praying, the angel came and said that God had heard his prayer. The angel Gabriel told Zacharias that he and Elisabeth would have a son who would grow up in the spirit and power of Elijah (Luke 1:8-17).

The history of the course of Abia is found in many ancient records. According to the sources, the first course of Abia served at the temple December 12 – 18 and the second course of Abia served June 13 – 19. Zacharias would've been serving in the second course. The course of Abia in 5 BC was completed on June 19 – a Friday. Zacharias' service at the temple would've ended that evening at sundown. He could not travel on the 20th because it was the Sabbath. Therefore, he would not have left Jerusalem until June 21st.

Zacharias and Elisabeth lived in the Judean Hills. It would have taken two or three days for this elderly man to walk from the temple to his home. He would have arrived home on June 23$^{rd}$ or 24$^{th}$. This means John the Baptist probably was conceived of Zacharias in Elisabeth's womb on June 23$^{rd}$ or June 24$^{th}$.

In the sixth month of Elisabeth's pregnancy (around December 23$^{rd}$ or 24$^{th}$), the angel Gabriel appeared to Mary in Nazareth. This means the conception of Jesus Christ in Mary's womb probably would've occurred on the night of December 24$^{th}$ – Christmas Eve according to our calendar. December 25$^{th}$ according to the Jewish calendar.

Life begins at conception and not at birth. Christmas came on December 25$^{th}$ at the time the life of Jesus Christ began in the womb of Mary.

## The Childbirth

What date did Mary give birth? If the calendar records are correct, and the historical date for the decree of Caesar Augustus is correct, then it was in the early fall not in the winter. The date for Jesus to be born was perfect – He was born on the first day of the Feast of Tabernacles, September 29, 4 BC.

According to the Prophet Zachariah, the king of Israel was to be worshiped by Gentiles at the Feast of Tabernacles (Zachariah 14:16). Jesus, the King of Israel, was born on the first day of the Feast of Tabernacles, the only feast day directly associated with Gentile worship and salvation.

The Apostle John wrote, *"And the Word was made flesh, and dwelt among us"* (John 1:14a). The Greek word for "dwelt" literally means "tabernacled." When God came to earth to tabernacle among mankind, He timed His arrival in the Bethlehem manger to coincide with the Feast of Tabernacles.

The Feast of Tabernacles has always been the most joyous of all the Jewish feasts. It is their feast of Thanksgiving. The total meaning of the Feast of Tabernacles will not be fulfilled until the Lord returns to tabernacle among men while He rules and reigns over the earth from Mount Zion in Jerusalem.

I, for one, am looking forward to that day.

How about you?

Should you celebrate Christmas on December 25th? It's as good a day as any. Yet, all the other days of the year are Christmas too, if you have Christ within you.

## The Caesar

The youth minister at First Baptist Church in Gainesville, Florida was giving his annual Christmas children's sermon. He said, "Bethlehem was a very small town. In fact, it was so small, I'll bet they didn't even have a Pizza Hut." A little boy jumped up and said, "Maybe they had a Little Caesar's!"

The first person mentioned in Luke's Christmas story was not a Jew, nor a shepherd, nor a wise man. He was the Roman Emperor, Caesar Augustus, also known as Octavius. He was the nephew of Julius Caesar and the first Emperor of the Roman Empire. Augustus ruled from 27 BC until his death in 14 AD. Caesar Augustus had a fascinating career that began the bloodiest civil wars of the Roman Republic, and continued beyond the victory over his archrival Marc Anthony, and culminated in a lengthy era of peace and prosperity.

Luke's readers would have picked up on the irony of the mention of Caesar in his Christmas story because Caesar Augustus claimed to be a god. Caesar was a man who said he was a god. Jesus was God Who became a man.

## The Census

*"(And this taxing was first made when Cyrenius was governor of Syria.) And all went to be taxed, every one into his own city."*

**Luke 2:2-3**

There is an old play on words that preachers often quote, "Bethlehem – where Mary and Joseph had to come to their census (senses)." This particular census would leave many cent-less.

The Romans conducted a census for two reasons. One was to draft people into the military. The other was for taxation. Since Jews were exempt from military service, the purpose of this census was to count heads for taxation.

The more things change, the more they stay the same. People hated the tax-man back then, and people hate the tax-man today. Several years ago, I got a certified letter from the IRS - the Internal Revenue Service. The letter said I had done something wrong on my 2005 Tax Return. The letter further said the IRS wanted to talk to me.

I was so nervous about talking to the IRS that I could thread a sewing machine with it running. I called the IRS phone number and talked to their automated machine for about 30 minutes. When I finally got a hold of a real human being, they told me there was no problem. It was their mistake. I thanked God Almighty because there are three places I never want to stand – at the Great White Throne Judgment, before my wife when she is mad, or before somebody at the IRS.

Two thousand years ago, Caesar Augustus ordered a census for tax purposes which set people in motion all over the world. This was the sovereign plan of God to get Mary and Joseph to the right place at the right time. Under normal circumstances, Jesus would have been born in Joseph and Mary's hometown of Nazareth. However, Caesar Augustus decreed a census for his empire. Since both Joseph and Mary were descendants of King David, they had to travel down to David's city, Bethlehem, located six miles southwest of Jerusalem.

Today, you may have problems in your life. Maybe you have prayed and asked God for deliverance, but nothing has happened. The lesson in this story is to just relax. Keep it in the hands of the Lord. His timing is best. His purposes are perfect. God is working right now in whatever is going on in your life. Stay strong. Stay focused on Jesus Christ. Just remember, *"All things work together for good to them that love God, to them who are the called according to his purpose"* (Romans 8:28).

The census took place when Cyrenius (aka Quirinius) was governor of Syria. Cyrenius served as governor of Syria from AD 6 – 9. He conducted a census in AD 6 (see Acts 5:37). However, Cyrenius served as governor of Syria on separate occasions. He served an earlier term from 6 – 4 BC which aligns with the date of Jesus' birth.

### The Couple

*"And Joseph also went up from Galilee, out of the city of Nazareth, into Judaea, unto the city of David, which is called Bethlehem; (because he was of the house and lineage of David:) To be taxed with Mary his espoused wife, being great with child."*

**Luke 2:4-5**

A teacher once asked a Sunday school class, "Why was Jesus born in Bethlehem?" A little boy raised his hand and replied, "Because his mother was there."

Bethlehem means the "house of bread." The Bread of Life (John 6:48) was born in the house of bread. The Hebrew word for bread is *lechem*. The place where Jesus first appeared in bodily form, contains the same word He spoke over the bread that represented His body at the first Lord's Supper.

However, Bethlehem has another name. It was known as Bethlehem Ephratah. Ephratah means "fruit of the vine." The place where Jesus first appeared in bodily form, contains the same word he spoke over the wine that represented His blood at the first Lord's Supper. Bethlehem Ephratah, the place where Jesus first appeared in flesh and blood contains the name of the symbols of His flesh and blood – bread and wine.

A little girl in a suburban Philadelphia Children's Church was asked where Jesus was born. She answered, "Philadelphia." The teacher said, "No, try again." The little girl said, "Pittsburgh." When the teacher again said that was a wrong answer, the child asked, "Where was it, then?" "Bethlehem," replied the teacher. "Oh," the little girl said, "I knew it was somewhere in Pennsylvania."

Mary was "great with child." That means she was very pregnant. She was getting ready to deliver. Why would she travel 90-miles if she was about to have a baby?

Today, 90-miles does not seem like a big deal. My daughter can drive 90-miles in about 45 minutes. Which reminds me, I need to make sure my life insurance policy is up to date before I ride with her again.

Ninety miles may not seem like much today, but back then, it was a big deal for Mary and Joseph. They traveled 90-miles over rough terrain. Most likely, Mary wouldn't have been able to walk. She probably rode a donkey. It would have taken 3 or 4 solid days of hard travel to get from Nazareth down to Bethlehem. Why would Mary make that journey?

### Pressure

The Roman government had been in a state of war and conquest for many years. They were broke. That is why Caesar ordered the census – so he could raise money by taxing the Roman Empire. If a person did not go and register within a certain time, they would be jailed. If Joseph did not go to Bethlehem, he would be thrown in jail and Mary could have been taken by the Romans and sold as a slave to pay their debt. They had no choice.

### Passion

There is little doubt Joseph deeply loved Mary. When he found out she was expecting a Child, he knew the Child wasn't his. He could only assume she had been unfaithful. Under Jewish Law, Joseph could have had Mary publicly humiliated or stoned to death. Yet he loved her so much, he decided he would put her away quietly. Even though he was hurt, he didn't want to hurt the woman he passionately loved.

As Joseph thought on these things, an angel appeared to him in a dream, and said, "*Joseph, thou son of David, fear not to take unto thee Mary thy wife: for that which is conceived in her is of the Holy Ghost.*" After the dream, Joseph then took Mary to be his wife.

When it came time to travel to Bethlehem, there was no way Joseph would leave Mary behind. He would never leave her alone in Nazareth to have the Baby when he wasn't there. He passionately loved her.

### Pregnancy

Mary was pregnant out of wedlock. Most likely, it had not been a good nine-months for her in Nazareth. In that time, a woman who was pregnant before her wedding was usually executed. Having a baby out of wedlock in that culture was a terrible scandal. She couldn't stay behind without Joseph to protect her.

### Prophecy

Mary and Joseph were Godly Jews. They would have been aware of the Old Testament prophecy which

23

said, *"But thou, Bethlehem Ephratah, though thou be lit-tle among the thousands of Judah, yet out of thee shall he come forth unto me that is to be ruler in Israel; whose goings forth have been from of old, from everlasting"* (Micah 5:2). They knew that the Messiah was to be born in Bethlehem. They must have recognized the hand of God in their situation.

Caesar unknowingly was fulfilling a 700-year-old prophecy when he ordered the census. The Messiah had to be born in Bethlehem when His mother and His foster father lived in Nazareth. God used a decree by Caesar to move Mary and Joseph to Bethlehem to fulfill prophecy. Seven hundred years before He was born, Micah prophe-sied that Jesus would be born in Bethlehem and God lit-erally moved the whole world to make it happen the way it was prophesied. When Mary and Joseph were in the right place, Jesus was born.

Today, you may believe that you are not in the right place in your life. Whatever your circumstance, if God has planted you there, it's the right place for the time being. God is at work wherever you are located. Pray and ask God to bloom you where you are planted.

God is in control of world events. If God is in con-trol of world events, how much more is He in control of your life?

# THE HUMBLE BIRTH
# OF THE SAVIOR

*"And so it was, that, while they were there, the days were accomplished that she should be delivered. And she brought forth her firstborn son, and wrapped him in swaddling clothes, and laid him in a manger; because there was no room for them in the inn."*

**Luke 2:6-7**

Mary brought forth *"her"* firstborn son. Notice the Bible does not say "their" firstborn son. Jesus Christ is the virgin born Son of God. Joseph is not the father.

The *"swaddling clothes"* were long cloth strips used to keep babies' limbs straight so they could grow properly. Babies in that time were rubbed down with olive oil and wrapped in strips of cloth.

Then Mary laid Him in a manger. A manger was a feeding trough used for cattle, sheep, donkeys, or horses. Archaeologists have discovered stone mangers in the horse stables of Ahab at Megiddo. They were cut out of limestone and were approximately three feet long, eighteen inches wide, and two feet deep.

There was no room for them *"in the inn."* Somebody sent me an email the other day with this question: Do you know why Jesus was born in a stable? It was because his parents had government healthcare.

I always believed that Bethlehem was full of mean old innkeepers who had all turned away a poor woman who was about to have a baby. Until, finally, Mary and Joseph came to an innkeeper who said they could sleep in the barn out back.

A few years ago, my family and I purchased a home in a small town in Southeast Kansas. When we arrived at the town, our house wasn't ready for us to occupy. We had to stay in a motel.

We went to the Sleep Inn, but they had no vacancy. We went to the Travel Lodge, but they had no vacancy. Went to the Rodeway Inn, but they had no vacancy. I asked the clerk at the Rodeway Inn why all the motel rooms were filled up. He told me there was a rodeo in town and every motel was booked solid. We had to travel to the next town to find a room. As we were driving out of town, one of our children said from the backseat, "Now I know how Mary and Joseph felt."

All my life, I had an image of Mary and Joseph running from the Holiday Inn to the Motel 6. I had a picture of them running from one hotel to another. That makes for a good story, but it is not true.

The truth is Joseph and Mary show up at David's family's plot of ground. Everybody who was a descendent of David had seven days to register and pay their taxes in Bethlehem. Over the centuries, there were many, many descendants of David. Bethlehem was full of people.

Joseph and Mary arrived at their relative's home and were turned away by their own family.

The word "inn" is the Greek word, *kataluma*. It is used two other times in the New Testament and both times it means a guestroom in a private home. Later, when the wise men come to visit, they are staying in a house. Every home had a small little guest room in the front of the house, but when Mary and Joseph arrived, the room was full. So, their relatives put them out behind the house in a cave where they kept animals. God, when He became a man, spent His first night in a nasty barn.

That night was filled with sweat, pain, blood, and cries as Mary reached up to heaven for help. The ground was cold and hard. The place smelled like manure and dusty hay. Joseph hurried to gather straw to make Mary a bed as her contractions intensified. He cleaned away spider webs to find a place to lay his wife.

As she gave birth, Joseph brushed the hair off Mary's brow and wiped the sweat off her face. He held her hand as donkeys and sheep watched. She pushed one last time and trembling calloused carpenter's hands grabbed God's Son, slippery with blood. The Lord Jesus Christ's first breath was taken in the cold damp air of a nasty smelly barn. The cry of the Baby in that cold night was the announcement that Jesus Christ was born.

King Jesus had arrived on planet earth.

Majesty was in the manger.

Do you want to get into the Christmas spirit? Cuddle a tiny baby close to you. Let those tiny fingers grab yours. Hold the little child against you. Feel the baby's complete dependence upon you. Experience the fragility of that precious little life and you will begin, in a small sense, to understand the incarnation. God poured Himself into just such a frail life and made it His own. He allowed Himself to be dependent upon His creation, to be at their mercy.

## HELLISH BLINDNESS
## OF THE SKEPTIC

The Christmas story could also be called the "Christmiss" story because someone in the story completely missed the birth of Christ. There was no room for them in the inn (the guestroom). There were thousands of people in Bethlehem because of the decree of Caesar. People had come back to their hometown and had found there was no room. Don't you think a room could have been made available? Imagine if whoever had answered the knock at the door had said, "There's no room here. Not even a spot on the floor. However, since your wife is having a baby. You can have my room. I will sleep outside in the barn." Sadly, that did not happen.

What was done to Christ that day was done through ignorance. They didn't know Mary was giving birth to the King of Kings. Back then, when Christ was turned away, it was done through ignorance. Today, people do the same thing through indifference. Today, our lives are so crowded, there is no room for Jesus.

There is no room for Jesus in our families. There is no room for Jesus in our jobs. There is no room for Jesus in our schools. There is no room for Jesus in our government. There is no room for Jesus in our lives. There is no room for Jesus anywhere.

It is heartbreaking – when Jesus was born there was no room in the inn, but there was room in a dungeon the night He was arrested. There was room on a pole where He was tied for the flesh to be beaten off His back with the Roman scourge. There was room on a cross. There was room between two thieves where He died in agony and shame.

Is there room for Him in your life?

The Lord Jesus Christ entered this world quietly in an out-of-the-way place. He was born in a barn. The King of all Glory had a homeless birth.

Years later, when Jesus was an adult, and toward the end of His ministry, a teacher declared that he would follow the Master anywhere. Jesus replied, *"Foxes have holes, and birds of the air have nests; but the Son of man hath not where to lay his head"* (Luke 9:58). The King of the Universe ended up the way He started – homeless.

However, the Baby in Bethlehem's manger came to find room for you. Before He went to the cross, the Lord Jesus Christ told His disciples, *"In my Father's house are many mansions: if it were not so, I would have told you. I go to prepare a place for you"* (John 14:2). Jesus has made a reservation for you at the inn that awaits in heaven. Homeless no more, Jesus will throw open the doors of heaven so that you will not be left out in the cold.

Several years ago, forty-two-year-old David Saunders waited on the driveway of his Hanover, Michigan home for his 4-year-old daughter, Danielle, to get off her school bus. A pickup truck was stopped behind the bus. David crossed the street to meet Danielle at the bus and then the two crossed the street together and stood in the Saunders' driveway.

Suddenly, David noticed that a car behind the bus was traveling too fast to stop safely before entering the crossing zone. The car swerved to avoid the pickup and went into the Saunders' driveway. Heading directly for them both, David grabbed his daughter by the arm and flung her away from himself into their front yard. He was then struck by the car – David Saunders was pronounced dead at the scene.

Danielle was treated for minor injuries at a nearby hospital and soon released. The 16-year-old driver and a 15-year-old passenger were not injured. Sheriff's Captain Tony Philipps said, "It was a heroic act by a father to save his child. He did everything he could, and in the process, he lost his own life."

Jesus, the Mighty God, came to earth to take the hit for you on the cross. Every year at Christmas time when I see the Baby in the manger, I can't help but picture Him 33 years later nailed to the cross. From the cradle to the cross – that was His destiny.

He was born to die for you.

# Chapter 2
# THE CHOIR

"Angels were active in every phase of the announcement and birth of Christ."

Dr. Bob Glaze

## Angels

*"Likewise, I say unto you, there is joy in the presence of the angels of God over one sinner that repenteth."*

**Luke 15:10**

One year, a young man went to Walmart to buy his wife a gift for Christmas. While he was there, he noticed an older man who he assumed to be a grandfather and his badly-behaved grandson. The grandfather had his hands full with the little kid who was screaming and carrying on. The little boy yelled, "I want some candy! I want some candy! I want some candy!" The old grandfather said in a soft voice, "Easy William, we won't be long…easy boy."

Suddenly, the little boy started screaming again, "I want some cookies! I want some cookies! I want some cookies!" The old grandfather calmly said, "It's okay William. Just a couple more minutes and we'll be out of here. Hang in there, boy."

At the checkout, the little boy was throwing things out of the shopping cart. He was screaming, "I want a toy! I want a toy! I want a toy!" The old grandfather said in a soft, controlled voice, "William, William, relax buddy. Don't get upset. We will be home in five minutes. Stay cool William."

The young man was very impressed. He checked out, walked outside, looked up, and saw the old grandfather loading his Walmart bags and the little boy in the car. The young man said, "Sir, it's none of my business, but you were amazing in there. I don't know how you did it. That whole time you kept your composure. No matter how loud and disruptive he got, you just calmly kept saying things would be okay. William is very lucky to have you as his granddad."

The old man said, "Thanks, but I'm William. This little brat is named Joey!"

The young man got the wrong message. When it comes to Christmas, it's important for us to get the message right because we are to be messengers.

After Jesus was born in Bethlehem, angels appeared and gave the message to the shepherds. The shepherds then shared the message. As Christian men and women, it is our responsibility to share the message – to share the Gospel – to share the good news that Jesus Christ was born of a virgin. That He lived a perfect, sinless life. That He died on an old rugged cross to pay for our sins. That He was buried. That three days later, He rose again. And all you must do is repent of your sins and believe on the Lord Jesus Christ and you will be saved. That's the Gospel. That's the message – we had better get it right.

After the Lord Jesus Christ was born, it was time for the birth announcement. God chose unusual messengers, angels, to deliver the birth announcement.

*"And suddenly there was with the angel a multitude of the heavenly host praising God, and saying, Glory to God in the highest, and on earth peace, good will toward men."*
**Luke 2:13**

A multitude of angels appeared with Gabriel to praise God. I believe the angel was Gabriel because he is called "'the' angel," as if he were the same angel that appeared in the chapter before – the angel Gabriel.

The word "angel" means messenger. These messengers from heaven have come to earth to let people know that the moment history has been building towards

35

has arrived. If you look closely at their message, you will find some wonderful things.

## AN ENCOURAGING
## MESSAGE

First, the message of the angels was an encouraging message. The world we live in today is in desperate need of encouragement. Discouragement is one of the biggest weapons in the devil's arsenal.

*"And there were in the same country shepherds abiding in the field, keeping watch over their flock by night. And, lo, the angel of the Lord came upon them, and the glory of the Lord shone round about them: and they were sore afraid."*

**Luke 2:8-9**

From the language, it seems the angel appeared out of the Shekinah glory of the Lord. "Shekinah" is a Hebrew word that literally means, "he caused to dwell." It was used to describe a divine visitation of the presence or dwelling of God on the earth. The Shekinah was first revealed when the Israelites left their captivity in Egypt. The Lord appeared in a cloudy pillar in the day and a fiery pillar by night (Exodus 13:20-22).

In Exodus 33, Moses said to God, *"I beseech thee, shew me thy glory."* God told him, *"Thou canst not see my face: for there shall no man see me, and live.*" So, God hid Moses in the cleft of a rock, covered him with His hand, and passed by. When God removed His hand, Moses only saw His back. God's back was so radiant and bright, it caused Moses face to reflect God's Shekinah. Moses shone so brightly when he came down from Mount Sinai, he had to cover his face with a veil.

In the New Testament, Jesus Christ was the dwelling place of God's glory (Colossians 2:9). He was the visible manifestation of God Himself in the second Person of the Trinity even though His glory was also veiled. The Apostle John said about Jesus coming into the world, "*In him was life; and the life was the light of men*" (John 1:4). Jesus is the "*light of the world*" (John 8:12). Christmas is all about lights.

This world is full of darkness. If you don't think the world is dark, just turn on the evening news: crime, murder, suicides, scandals, shootings, drug abuse, child abuse, terrorism, war, political fighting, greed… The world is a mess. The mess the world is in is not God's fault. God did not create the world to be this dark.

Christmas is the story of God's solution to the darkness. It is the story of how God brought light back to our dark world. John refers to Jesus as "*the light*."

Jesus who was with God in the very beginning of all creation, is the light that has come to conquer the darkness. Jesus came because we needed the light that only He could bring. He is our only hope against the darkness.

Several years ago, I visited Carlsbad Caverns in southern New Mexico. Eight-hundred-thirty-feet down, we came to what is called "The King's Palace." There, the tour guide turned off the lights. Suddenly we were plunged into complete and utter darkness. She told us ahead of time that the lights were going to be turned off. When it happened, I waved my hand in front of my face. There was such an absence of light that I could literally not see my hand – or anything else. It was complete and utter darkness.

Without Christmas, our world would be in complete and utter darkness. We would be lost and wandering forever, in the absence of any light at all. Thankfully Jesus is the light of the world.

In December of 1997, the *Fort Scott Tribune*, a newspaper in Fort Scott, Kansas made a typo when announcing the winner of the city Christmas lighting contest. The article read, "The winners for the 1997 Light Up Fort Scott Christmas lighting contest (sponsored by the Kiwanis Pioneers) have been announced. Signs will be placed in the sinners' yards during the Christmas season to recognize their efforts."

Of course, the newspaper meant to say, "winners," not "sinners." Still, they printed the truth. We are all sinners. You are a sinner, so am I. But Christ came into the world to save sinners.

Here is the real meaning of Christmas. It is not about Santa. It is not about gifts. It isn't even about getting together with your family. Christmas is all about the lights – the reminder that Jesus, the Light of the World, has come to save you from the dark.

Every time you see a Christmas light this year, I hope you will see more than lights. I hope you see Jesus.

*"And the angel said unto them, Fear not: for, behold, I bring you good tidings of great joy, which shall be to all people."*

**Luke 2:10**

The shepherds were afraid. So, the angel said to them, "Fear not." Over 365 times in the Bible, you find some form of the phrase "fear not." The Bible teaches that God will take care of you. God will see you all the way home. You are to fear not. You don't live from a position of fear. You live from a position of faith. Fear not.

One day, Grandma sent her grandson, Johnny, down to the creek to get a bucket of water. As Johnny was dipping the bucket into the water, he saw two big eyes looking back at him. Floating there in the creek was a giant alligator. Johnny dropped the bucket and ran as fast as he could back to Grandma's kitchen.

When he got back to the house, Grandma said, "Johnny, where's my bucket? Where's my water?" Johnny said, "Grandma, I can't get any water from that creek. There's a big alligator down there." Grandma said, "Now don't you mind that gator. He's been there for a few years now and he's never hurt no one. Why he's probably as scared of you as you are of him." Johnny said, "Well Grandma, if he's as scared of me as I am of him, then that water ain't fit to drink!"

Are you like Johnny? Are you afraid of everything you can't control? God tells you to "fear not."

Do you worry when you turn on the news and see the world falling apart? God says, "Fear not." Are you having trouble making ends meet? God says, "Fear not." Is your job stressful? God says, "Fear not." Do you have health concerns? God says, "Fear not." Are you having family problems? God says, "Fear not." When it seems like your future is uncertain, God says, "Fear not."

When we hear certain words we immediately think of Christmas – Advent, candy canes, fruitcake, elves, holly, mistletoe, poinsettias, red-nosed reindeer, sleigh bells, and wreaths. There may be other reminders, depending on your own experiences and memories.

When we turn to the Bible, there are other words which we associate with the birth of our Savior – Angels, wise men, shepherds, manger, the star, Bethlehem, gold, frankincense, and myrrh just to name a few. It is certainly appropriate that we should have so many mental associations with Christmas.

However, there is a little word here in the Christmas story which may be the most important when it comes to understanding what happened when God became one of us. For the most part, this word has been overlooked.

In fact, some of the modern translations just leave it out altogether, as if the word were not very important at all. Ten times in the first two chapters of Luke, we find this word in the original language. Sometimes it is translated as "lo," but most of the time it appears as "behold." This little word tells us that the story of Christmas is amazing.

In the New Testament, "behold" is used as an interjection, or an exclamation. Examples of exclamations in English would be "Hey!" or "Oh!" or "Ouch!" It is what you might say if you want to make certain someone does not miss something, such as in "Hey! Look at this!"

The original word used here carries a lot of intense emotion, so it can be difficult to translate. Sometimes it has the idea of "pay attention to this," but at least one scholar has suggested that another appropriate English word would be, "Wow!"

The Apostle Paul wrote to the church in Corinth, *"Therefore if any man be in Christ, he is a new creature: old things are passed away; behold, all things are become new"* (2 Corinthians 5:17) Paul said that Christ has made us new, and he says, "Wow!"

At the exact moment Jesus died on the cross, there was an incredible earthquake. *"And, behold, the veil of the temple was rent in twain from the top to the bottom; and the earth did quake, and the rocks rent"* (Matthew 27:51).

At the very moment when Jesus died on the cross, the veil of the temple was torn in two – beginning at the top and going to the bottom. This was a significant thing to happen, so Matthew says, "Behold" or "Wow!"

The word "behold" or "wow" is found all throughout the Christmas story. Gabriel told Mary she was going to give birth to the Messiah. The angel said to her, "Behold" Wow! (Luke 1:31)

Mary responded to Gabriel's announcement when she said, "Behold" Wow! (Luke 1:38; 48).

Doesn't it make sense? Doesn't it fit, that when she heard what God was going to do Mary would respond with "Wow!" She later meditated on what this would mean, and she said "Wow! From henceforth all generations shall call me blessed."

Mary went to visit her cousin Elisabeth who was pregnant with John the Baptist. Mary arrived and greeted Elisabeth who responded with, "Wow!"

The angel said, *"Fear not: for, behold, I bring you good tidings of great joy, which shall be to all people"* The angel said, "Fear not. Wow! I bring you good news of great joy."

We make a mistake when we run across the word "behold" and see it as a ho-hum expression to just fill up space. We are also mistaken when we imagine the voice of the angel Gabriel sharing this amazing news, and blaring it out in a bold ground shaking, commanding voice, "BEHOLD!" It seems to me that we should hear the word as being spoken in a worshipful, reverent, breathless, awestruck manner, "Behold! Wow!"

The angel said to them, "*Fear not: for, behold, I bring you good tidings of great joy, which shall be to all people. For unto you is born this day in the city of David a Saviour, which is Christ the Lord.*"

Wow!

## AN EXCLUSIVE MESSAGE

*"For unto you is born this day in the city of David a Saviour, which is Christ the Lord."*

**Luke 2:11**

The word "Christ" is the Greek equivalent of the Hebrew word "Messiah. It means "anointed one." In ancient times, kings were inaugurated by anointing. The Messiah was the promised King of David's line.

The angel tells the shepherds that Christ the Lord is born "unto you." Born to you. Salvation is exclusive to the individual. It is personal.

The angel continues, "*Ye shall find the babe wrapped in swaddling clothes.*" You shall find the Baby. The message from heaven to you is that you can personally have a heart to heart relationship with God. The Gospel is for the whole world, but it is also exclusive to you as an individual. You can be in a personal, intimate fellowship with the living Christ. The angel says to the shepherds the message is to you – you will personally find the baby wrapped in swaddling clothes. The only way you can be saved is for you personally to receive the message that eternal life is in Christ alone.

## AN ESSENTIAL
## MESSAGE

*"And this shall be a sign unto you; Ye shall find the babe wrapped in swaddling clothes, lying in a manger."*
**Luke 2:12**

When angels speak in the Bible, they often speak in short, urgent commands. The angel says the shepherds will find a sign. In other words, "Go now." Don't wait. There is a heaven. There is a hell. There may be no tomorrow. Today is the day of salvation. This is your moment. God has brought you to this place. Trust Him now. Get saved now. Turn to Christ now. Be born again now.

You never know when your life will end. Anthony Fernando, a twenty-one-year-old man living in Colombo, Sri Lanka, went fishing one day off the coast of the island. He had no idea he would never make it back alive. A forktail gar fish jumped out of the water and cut him on the neck with its tail. He bled to death before a fellow fisherman could get him to a hospital.

Lance Foster, a twenty-three-year-old student at the University of Kansas was studying at his desk one night. Little did he know he would be dead a few minutes later. Foster became thirsty and decided to walk down the hallway to get something to drink. He put his money in the machine, but the drink didn't come out. When he rocked the vending machine back and forth to get the can of soda, it fell on top of him. He died from internal injuries shortly thereafter.

If you would have told Ali-Asghar Ahani he would be shot to death by a snake, he wouldn't have believed it. But it happened. Although he could have shot the snake, this man from Iran was trying to capture it alive. When he pressed the butt of his shotgun behind its head, the snake coiled itself around the gun. With its tail thrashing, the snake pulled the trigger, firing one of the barrels and shooting Ahani in the head.

Not one of them knew or even imagined that death was just moments away. Death can come unexpectedly to anyone. If the Lord tarries, you are going to die. Have you ever thought about how you will die? Will you be cut by a fish tail? Crushed by a soda machine? Shot by a snake? Maybe your heart will just stop beating. You probably won't be able to predict how or when your death will occur. Nevertheless, you have an appointment with death, and you need to be prepared.

This is an essential message. You are not promised tomorrow. If you are reading this and you are without Jesus Christ, get saved today.

*"And suddenly there was with the angel a multitude of the heavenly host praising God, and saying, Glory to God in the highest, and on earth peace, good will toward men."*
**Luke 2:13-14**

"Host" was a military word that was used for a band of soldiers. Here the heavenly army was on a different kind of mission. They had come to announce the birth of the King of Kings.

The angels sang, *"Glory to God in the highest, and on earth peace."* The Greek word for "peace" is *eirēnē*, and is similar to the Hebrew word *Shalom*. Shalom means "peace, wholeness, or completeness." Shalom means "well-being, harmony, and security."

Life was difficult at that time just as it is today. Taxes were high, unemployment was high, morals were slipping lower, and the military state was in control. Roman law, Greek philosophy, and even Jewish religion could not bring peace to men's hearts. Then, God sent His Son.

Today, peace is still rare. People need peace. Homes need peace. Neighborhoods need peace. Cities need peace. Countries need peace. This world needs peace. You need peace. Christ came to give you peace.

During dinner one evening, the youngest member of the family, a four-year-old boy, stood up in his chair and screamed, "PASS THE BUTTER!" His mother was shocked at his behavior and said, "No supper for you until you learn some manners. Get down and go to your room."

"But…" the little boy began.

"No 'but's' about it. Go to your room."

Later, the father called the entire family into the living room. "I had the tape recorder turned on during dinner tonight," he said. "I want us to listen to ourselves as we really are." When he turned on the recording, they all heard themselves talking at the same time. Amid the chatter, the little boy said, "Please pass the butter." Later, "Would somebody please pass the butter?" And finally, "PASS THE BUTTER!"

No one was listening.

Are you listening to what God is trying to say to you this Christmas? Can you hush the noise and hear the angels sing? Can you hush the noise of inner conflict in your heart? Can you hush the noise of guilt? Can you hush the noise of bitterness and long-standing resentments? Can you hush the noise and hear the message of peace?

In a world like ours, and in the time like ours, it is important for us to hush the noise and listen to what God is trying to tell you this Christmas.

The angels sang, *"Glory to God in the highest, and on earth peace, good will toward men."* When God created the world, He demonstrated His power. When God washed the earth away at the flood, He demonstrated His justice. When Jesus was born in Bethlehem's manger, God demonstrated His good will to men. Through the birth of Christ, God said, "I want to save you. I want to have a relationship with you. I sent my Son because I love you."

The angels brought an essential message. Angels were fascinated by Jesus. Angels were always around Jesus. Angels were there when Jesus was born. Angels ministered to Jesus when He walked the earth. Angels were there when Jesus died. Angels were there when Jesus rose from the dead. Angels were there when He ascended. Angels are surrounding Him in heaven right now praising Him. And one day, Jesus is going to descend through the clouds to come back to earth and all the armies of angels are coming back with Him.

You, like the angels, should be fascinated with Jesus. Don't be fascinated by a denomination. Don't be fascinated by preachers. Don't be fascinated by personalities. Just be fascinated about Jesus. Be fascinated about His words. Be fascinated about His miracles. Be fascinated about His teachings. Be fascinated about His Gospel.

You should be fascinated about and in love with Jesus Christ.

# Chapter 3
# THE CARETAKERS

"He who has not Christmas in his heart will
never find it under a tree."

Roy L. Smith

## Shepherds

*"I am the good shepherd: the good shepherd giveth his
life for the sheep."*

**John 10:11**

B ack in May of 2007, Queen Elizabeth II visited the
United States. When the Queen of England travels,
she travels in style. On this trip, Elizabeth brought four
thousand pounds of luggage which included two outfits
for every occasion, a mourning outfit in case someone
died, 40 pints of plasma, and white kid-leather toilet seat
covers. She also brought along her own hairdresser, two

valets, and a host of other attendants. It was estimated that Elizabeth's trip cost 20 million dollars.

In meek contrast, God's visit to earth took place in a barn with nowhere to lay the newborn King but in a feed trough. Jesus had no attendants present. His arrival was only noticed by society's outcasts, the shepherds.

*The Mishnah* was the first written record of Jewish oral traditions. It is also known as the "Oral Torah." *The Mishnah* stipulated that all the flocks be kept in the wilderness, except the flocks used for the temple services which were kept at Bethlehem. These shepherds had the responsibility of being the caretakers of the sacrificial lambs, many of which would become Passover lambs, when the ultimate Passover Lamb was born.

## EXTRAORDINARY MESSENGERS

*"And it came to pass, as the angels were gone away from them into heaven, the shepherds said one to another, Let us now go even unto Bethlehem, and see this thing which is come to pass, which the Lord hath made known unto us."*

**Luke 2:15**

What is the best news you have ever received? How did you react when you heard it? Did it produce excitement, or did it bring peace? Was there a feeling of exhilaration, or did a calm feeling settle over you? Perhaps you have experienced some or all these emotions and maybe even more.

There have been times when I received wonderful news in my life. It was wonderful news, when my wife, Amanda, said "yes" to marrying me. It was wonderful news when Amanda said, "We are going to have a baby" – all three times. It was wonderful news, when I was serving in the U.S. Army in a war far from home and the commander came and said, "We are going home." Each of those incidents were good news.

However, the best news you or I have ever received pales in comparison to the news that the angel gave to the shepherds some two-thousand or so years ago. The angel said, *"Fear not: for, behold, I bring you good tidings of great joy, which shall be to all people. For unto you is born this day in the city of David a Saviour, which is Christ the Lord."* The shepherds received the best news anyone in the world had ever received – God had come to earth in the Person of Jesus Christ.

On July 29, 1969, astronaut Neil Armstrong climbed down a ladder and put his feet on the surface of the moon. In an address, President Richard Nixon said, "The greatest event in human history occurred when man first put his foot on the moon." Astronaut Hale Irwin responded to Nixon's comments, "The most significant achievement of our age is not that man stood on the moon, but rather that God in Christ stood on the earth." That is the greatest news in all of history.

The term "first responders" is used to describe someone who is trained to respond to an emergency. It is used to describe police officers, firemen, and emergency medical technicians. "First responders" could also be used to describe the shepherds. They were the first to respond and proclaim the arrival of the Messiah.

Shepherds were despised in the time of Jesus, but they were not always despised. In the Old Testament, David was a shepherd. Moses was a shepherd. Being a shepherd was a wonderful profession in the Old Testament, but not in the day of Christ. The Pharisees, the Sadducees, and the religious rulers despised shepherds because they couldn't keep all their religious rules. In order to be religiously pure, you had to do all this ceremonial washing, and keep all these rules. Shepherds had to work outside in the fields. They couldn't keep all these rules.

Religion, man-made tradition, ruins people. Religion is man's attempt to be right with God with his own good works. Religion is man trying to earn his way into heaven. Religion is spelled D-O. Christianity is spelled D-O-N-E.

People can sit in church their entire life and die and go to hell because they are blinded by the human traditions of men. They are blinded by religion.

The shepherds outside of Bethlehem were tending the very flocks that were used in the sacrifices of

Jerusalem. These shepherds took care of the lambs that were offered in the name of religion, but they were despised and not allowed in the temple. God sent the message to these shepherds because they had not been ruined by religion.

*"And this shall be a sign unto you; Ye shall find the babe wrapped in swaddling clothes, lying in a manger."*

**Luke 2:12**

A baby "wrapped in swaddling clothes, lying in a manger" sounds strange to us today. However, this would not have sounded strange to the shepherds.

In Genesis 35:21 we read, *"And Israel journeyed, and spread his tent beyond the tower of Eder."* This passage has to do with the burial of Jacob's wife, Rachel. Rachel was buried in Bethlehem (Genesis 35:19). After his wife's burial, Jacob camped near Bethlehem in a place beyond what the Hebrew calls *"Migdal Eder"* or the Tower of Eder.

The Tower of Eder was originally built as a military outpost outside of Bethlehem for the protection of Jerusalem located six miles away. Later, King Solomon moved the military garrison and changed the name of the Tower of Eder to the Tower of the Flock because it was used by the shepherds.

The Tower of the Flock was a three-story structure. The shepherds would watch over their flocks from the top story, the second story was used for storage, and the bottom story was used as a birthing chamber. Each time an ewe was ready to give birth, the shepherds would take her out of the valley and up the hill to the Tower of the Flock. When the ewe delivered, the baby lamb would be cleaned up and wrapped with swaddling clothes to restrict it from moving.

After the newborn lamb was swaddled, it would be carried into the inner chamber of the Tower of the Flock. There, the lamb would be laid inside a stone manger. The little lamb remained in the manger until he could be inspected for spot or blemish by the chief shepherd. If the lamb was acceptable, it would be taken back to its mother and back to the flock. As the lamb grew, if it developed no spot or blemish, it would be used as a sacrifice in the Temple.

The shepherds knew exactly what to look for when they heard the angel say that they would find a baby "wrapped in swaddling clothes, lying in a manger." The Lord Jesus Christ was born in the shadow of the Tower of the Flock. He was born in the same place as the sacrificial lambs. He was wrapped in the same cloths as the sacrificial lambs. He was laid in the same kind of manger as the sacrificial lambs. No wonder John the Baptist said about Him, "Behold the Lamb of God, which taketh away the sin of the world" (John 1:29b).

Seven-hundred years before Jesus was born, the prophet Micah, under the inspiration of the Holy Spirit wrote, "But thou, Bethlehem Ephratah, though thou be little among the thousands of Judah, yet out of thee shall he come forth unto me that is to be ruler in Israel; whose goings forth have been from of old, from everlasting." This amazing prophecy predicts the exact birthplace of the Messiah. But Micah digs down deeper when he writes, "And thou, O tower of the flock, the strong hold of the daughter of Zion, unto thee shall it come, even the first dominion; the kingdom shall come to the daughter of Jerusalem" (Micah 4:8). Seven-hundred years before His birth, Micah said Jesus would be born in Bethlehem, specifically mentioning the Tower of the Flock. Incredible.

A four-year-old girl often forgot to close the door when coming in from outside. Finally, her father scolded her, "Shut that door! Were you born in a barn?"

She looked at her father and replied softly, "No, but Jesus was."

Jesus was born in a barn. Mary had a little Lamb in a barn. She wrapped the Lamb in swaddling clothes and placed Him in a stone manger. When the Bethlehem shepherds came to inspect the Lamb, they found Him lying in the manger.

*"And they came with haste, and found Mary, and Joseph, and the babe lying in a manger."*

**Luke 2:16**

The shepherds came with haste. They were in a hurry. They came with haste and found. They found. That means they were searching.

Have you been searching your entire life? You thought your search had ended in a relationship, but that was a disaster. You thought your search had ended in a job, but that didn't work out. You thought your search had ended in a pill, something you sniffed up your nose, or in a bottle, but all that only left you depressed and miserable. You thought your search had ended in money, but that came up empty.

Today, if you will humble yourself, your search can be over. The only one Who can satisfy the longing and emptiness of your soul is Jesus Christ.

## EXCITED MESSENGERS

*"And when they had seen it, they made known abroad the saying which was told them concerning this child."*

**Luke 2:17**

The shepherds shared the message. They shared the good news that Jesus Christ was born. They didn't worry about how it was received. They didn't worry if people believed it. They didn't worry if people accepted it. Their job was to just deliver the message. That's what God has called us to do. It's not complicated. All you must do is tell people about your experience with Jesus Christ and leave the results in the hands of God.

They were excited about the message. I was going to hell, but now I am saved. That's something to get excited about. There was a load of sin crushing me, and now it is lifted off me. That's something to get excited about. My heart was empty and now it's full of Jesus. That's something to get excited about. When I die, I'm not going to die. That's something to get excited about. One day, I will stand in the eternal presence of Jesus Christ. That's something to get excited about. One day, I will see Him face to face. That's something to get excited about. God loved me so much that He sent His Son. That's something to get excited about. I am saved. That's something to get excited about.

Are you excited?

*"And all they that heard it wondered at those things which were told them by the shepherds."*
**Luke 2:18**

Two-thousand years ago, shepherds were not permitted to testify in court, but God used some humble shepherds to be the first human witnesses that prophecy had been fulfilled and the Messiah had been born. God used shepherds because they would understand that the Savior, lying in the quiet manger, was to be the Lamb of God. As the Lamb, He would die for the sins of the world.

He died for these very shepherds. God used shepherds, who cared for the young lambs, who sat through cold dark nights in the fields to guard and protect their flocks, because they understood the shepherd's heart of the Father and what it meant for Him to give His one Lamb for all.

The shepherds became the first evangelists by sharing the good news. The people who heard them "wondered" at the things the shepherds said. They were amazed the Messiah should be born in a stable and not in a palace, and angels should bring news of His birth to poor shepherds and not to the chief priests.

*"But Mary kept all these things, and pondered them in her heart."*

**Luke 2:19**

Several years ago, a young mother named Susan was released from the hospital after extensive rounds of therapy failed to turn back the progress of a deadly disease. Confined to her bed at home, she received regular visits from her physician, but she couldn't work up the courage to explain her illness to her six-year-old daughter.

One morning, the little girl overheard the doctor speaking with her mother and father. "I'll be frank with you, Susan," the physician said. "You don't have much time. I don't think you'll survive the autumn." A short while later, Susan glanced out the bedroom window and saw something that nearly broke her heart. She watched as her daughter bent to pick up the leaves that had begun to fall in the September breeze; and then, as if to foil the force of gravity itself, the little girl worked to scotch-tape each leaf back on a branch. She was trying to keep autumn from coming.

I wonder sometimes if Mary wished she could do something like that. Mary "kept" and "pondered" in her heart that her Baby was the Messiah. As she raised Jesus and saw Him grow and began to understand more and more of His mission here on earth, she must have wanted to turn back the clock. She knew that He was born to be the Savior of the world.

Mary "kept" all these things and "pondered" them in her heart. The word for "kept" means she "preserved" them in her heart. The word for "pondered" literally means "to throw together." Mary absorbed all that was happening around her and threw all the images and sounds and smells together to create a treasure in her heart.

Are you storing up, preserving, the treasures of Christmas in your heart?

In 1984, Jerry Falwell called singer, songwriter, Mark Lowry and asked him to write the script for Liberty University's annual Christmas program. Lowry was working on the program when he had a conversation with his mother. She said, "If anyone on earth knew for sure that Jesus was virgin born – Mary knew!" His mother's statement stuck with Lowry. He began writing a list of questions he would like to ask Mary if he could sit down with her. The questions Lowry wrote eventually became the wonderful Christmas song, *Mary, Did You Know?*

One of the lyrics of *Mary, Did You Know?* asks the question, "Mary, did you know that your baby boy is heaven's perfect lamb?"

Mary knew.

She knew that His hands so tiny on his birth night, would one day be pierced in two by nails.

She knew that Jesus was born to be the sacrificial Lamb to take away the sins of the world, and she "kept" and "pondered" it in her heart.

## EVERYDAY MESSENGERS

*"And the shepherds returned, glorifying and praising God for all the things that they had heard and seen, as it was told unto them."*

**Luke 2:20**

The shepherds returned. They returned to their jobs – to being shepherds. It was an old job, but they were new men. Now they had Jesus in their hearts and praise on their lips.

God wants you to go back to your job tomorrow. God wants you to go to your classroom. God wants you to go back to your life.

You may be thinking, "I've got an ordinary life." Quit thinking like that! You are a messenger of God. Our responsibility is to make Christ known wherever we might be. Go out and be a new man, a new woman, full of the Lord. One of the marks of a genuine Christian is a joyful confession of faith. An everyday place becomes an extraordinary place when there is a believer there full of Christ.

Don Bakely once pastored a church in urban Camden, New Jersey. At the time he pastored the church, Camden was named the nation's most dangerous city. He was especially concerned about a man named "Big Mart." One day Pastor Bakely was sitting in his church office, when he heard a commotion outside. He heard profanity, shouting, a loud argument. The argument was between Ella, the church secretary, and Big Mart. Big Mart was calling Ella a vile and obscene name. Before the pastor could respond, Ella came storming into his office.

She said, "Did you hear what that young man called me out there?" When he replied that he had, Ella asked, "Well, what are you going to do about it?" Pastor Bakely said, "That's a good question, Ella – a really good question. But the real question is what are you going to do about it?"

Ella had not expected that kind of an answer, but she regrouped and with some exasperation she said, "I guess I want you to go out there and throw him out." Pastor Bakely quickly replied, "Ella, I had been working for six weeks to get him in here. You want me to throw him out on the first day?"

The pastor continued, "Ella, let me tell you a story: it's a true story: then I want you to go home and think about it."

"When Big Mart was a little boy, his dad came home one night in a rage and began to beat up his mother. In a violent frenzy, he shoved the children into the room, closed the door, and forced them to watch while he killed their mother. He then took a paring knife and cut her head off her dead body. He decapitated their mother in front of those children. When Big Mart could not stand it anymore, he broke for the door and got out, but when he reached the top of the stairs, his father threw his mother's head and hit him in the back. The force of the blow knocked Big Mart down the stairs. When he woke up, he was lying on his mother's head. That's Big Mart. That's the guy you met out there. That's the guy who called you that name."

Ella didn't say a word. She turned and walked out the door, but she was back in 20 minutes. She walked over to the pastor's desk and looked at him. The pastor said, "Well?" And she said, "I guess I'm going to have to learn how to get cussed out."

Are there any "Big Mart's" in your life? How do you relate to them? Do you have a burden deep in your soul for them?

The good news of great joy is not just for church people. It's not just for "good people." The good news of great joy is for all people..." Rich people. Poor people. People who struggle to make ends meet. People with serious health issues. People who are healthy and strong. Single people. Divorced people. Married. Widowed. Educated. Uneducated. Conservative. Liberal. Young. Old. Black. White. Beautiful. Ugly. All people.

The good news of great joy is for all people.

How do you respond to the news?

The shepherds are a great example of how to respond. First, we should believe it. When the angels finished delivering their good news, the shepherds believed. They didn't argue among themselves, question what the angel had said, or try to understand what the angel had said. They just believed.

One important, basic response we should have to this good news of great joy is to believe it. Simply believe it.

Now, to believe something doesn't mean we have to understand it. I don't understand how God could become a man, but I believe it. I don't understand how Jesus could be born of a virgin, but I believe it. I responded to this good news by simply believing it. That is called faith. It was the same faith that enabled me to trust Jesus for my salvation.

In the realm of faith, there are no "if's." "If God does such and such, I'll believe him." "If I could understand it, I'd believe it." That's not faith.

Our second response to the good news is obey it. The angel told the shepherds the Christ Child will be found in the city of David. The message was so important to the shepherds that they hurried and obeyed without haste.

The third response to this good news is to tell it. When the shepherds saw the Christ Child, they began to share with others this good news of great joy. They told exactly what they had heard, and exactly what they had seen. Once they had seen the Christ Child, they could hardly speak of anything else.

I believe one of the reasons why there are not more people witnessing for Christ is because many who claim to be believers have not truly experienced Christ. You can't be a witness to something if you've never experienced it. But those of us who do believe and those who do obey – we are the ones commanded to be faithful witnesses.

What should you say? Just tell what you have seen and heard in your life as a Christian. Tell what Christ has done for you in the past. Tell what Christ is doing right now in the present. Tell what Christ will do for you in the future.

Respond to the good news of great joy by making this news known to others.

# Chapter 4
# THE CHOSEN

"She must be a virgin, that the glory of God
might be miraculously demonstrated."

Dr. David Jeremiah

## Mary

*"And I will put enmity between thee and the woman, and
between thy seed and her seed; it shall bruise thy head,
and thou shalt bruise his heel."*

**Genesis 3:15**

A little girl came home from Sunday school trium-
phantly waving a paper over her head. "Mommy!"
she said. "My teacher says I drew the most unusual
Christmas picture she has ever seen." The mother studied
the picture for a moment and concluded it was indeed a
unique picture of the Nativity scene. She said to her

daughter, "This is wonderfully drawn, but why have you made all of them riding in an airplane?" The little girl looked at her mother with a hint of disappointment that the pictures meaning was not obvious and said, "Well that's because they took their flight into Egypt."

"Oh, of course... But who is that mean looking man at the front of the airplane?"

"That's Pontius, the Pilot!" The girl said, now visibly impatient.

"I see. And here you have Mary, Joseph, and the baby," the mother said. She studied the picture silently for a moment and summoned the courage to ask, "But who is the overweight man sitting behind Mary?"

Her daughter said, "That's Round John Virgin, of course."

How do you view Mary? Are you like this little girl? Do you have a skewed perspective? I have been known to eat so much at Christmas time that I am beginning to see myself as Round John Virgin.

A man had more people coming over for Christmas than usual. He went looking for a turkey and was looking through the frozen section but couldn't find one big enough. So, he asked one of the extra Christmas staff, "Do these turkeys get any bigger?" "No, Sir," was the reply, "They're dead."

At Christmas, my wife works to make sure Christmas dinner is perfect and that everyone has enough to eat.

Truthfully, most people eat way too much at Christmas. The average person will gain six pounds over Christmas.

However, Christmas is not about gaining weight, it's about losing what weighs you down. Christ came to give you life and life more abundantly (John 10:10). Christ came so you can cast all your cares on Him because He cares for you (1 Peter 5:7). Whatever concerns or worries you may have this Christmas – you can bring them to God.

Sadly, most people have a distorted view of the Christmas story – especially when it comes to Mary.

One Christmas, when I was a little boy, I reached in my stocking and found a red plastic egg. The egg contained a little rubbery glob called "Silly Putty." With all the electronic gadgets they have today, kids have no interest in something as simple as Silly Putty, but in when I was a kid, it was something I was fascinated with.

One of my favorite things to do with Silly Putty was to flatten it and press it on the Sunday funnies in the newspaper or on a comic book page. The Silly Putty was sticky enough to pull the color print off the newspaper or the comic book page. Then Alley Oop, Dick Tracy, Superman, or whoever literally became putty in my hands.

Once I used Silly Putty and captured the image of Spider-man from a comic book. I pulled on the Silly Putty and stretched Spider-man out until he was tall and thin. Next, I crunched him down until he was squatty and fat.

Finally, I twisted him until he was distorted beyond recognition.

The very same thing has been done to Mary, the mother of the Lord Jesus Christ. She has been pulled, stretched, and distorted over the centuries until she is difficult to recognized. Mary has been "putty" in the hands of those who have pulled her out of all biblical proportions.

Some teach that Mary was immaculately conceived without sin. They believe that for Jesus to be conceived without sin, Mary would have to be without sin. However, that just pushes the problem back a generation because for Mary to be without sin, her parents would have to be without sin, and her grandparents, and her great-grandparents, and so on. You would have to keep on going back to each generation. The conception of Jesus Christ was a miracle. Jesus was conceived in Mary without a human father through which the sin nature comes.

Some believe Mary was bodily taken up to heaven. If you don't sin, then it stands to reason you don't die. So, many believe Mary was taken alive into heaven. Some even believe Mary is the queen of heaven. However, these beliefs have no basis in Scripture.

Some believe in praying to Mary. By praying to Mary and asking her to intercede on their behalf with God, they are assigning deity to her. While they believe Jesus Christ is the "Mediator;" they also believe Mary is the "Co-Mediator" or the feminine "Mediatrix." Therefore, they pray to Mary. However, there is no biblical basis for making Mary the Co-Mediator. In fact, the Bible contradicts this belief when it says, "For there is one God, and one mediator between God and men, the man Christ Jesus" (1 Timothy 2:5).

Babe Pinelli was a famous professional baseball umpire. In 1935, Pinelli was told he should not call a strike on the legendary baseball player, Babe Ruth, whose career was winding down with the Boston Braves. When a close pitch went by that Ruth didn't swing at, Pinelli called him out with a strike. The crowd in the stadium booed at their disapproval of the call. Babe Ruth turned to the umpire and said, "There's 40,000 people in this park that know that was a ball tomato-head!" Pinelli said, "Maybe so Babe, but mine is the only opinion that counts."

It is true in baseball that the umpire has the only opinion that counts. But in life, God has the only opinion that counts. The Bible has the final say-so on these matters. Let's look at what God says about Mary in the Holy Bible.

*"And Mary said, My soul doth magnify the Lord, And my spirit hath rejoiced in God my Saviour."*
**Luke 1:46-47**

Mary was not sinless. She knew she needed a Savior. She knew she was a sinner like everyone else. The Bible clearly says, Mary needed a Savior.

*"Then Joseph being raised from sleep did as the angel of the Lord had bidden him, and took unto him his wife: And knew her not till she had brought forth her firstborn son: and he called his name JESUS."*

**Matthew 1:24-25**

When author Donald Dugan's daughter, Nancy, was four-years-old, he decided to tell her what Christmas was all about. He and his wife told Nancy about the real meaning of Christmas and why they celebrated it. That Christmas was special to little Nancy. She had a wonderful day and received many presents and toys. A few days later, Nancy was talking with her older sister about what a great Christmas she had, and said, "I sure hope Joseph and Mary have another baby."

Mary and Joseph did have children of their own. Mary was not perpetually a virgin. Joseph did not know her until after the birth of Jesus. It was then they had a normal husband and wife relationship and had other children.

The Bible calls Jesus, Mary's "firstborn son" (Matthew 1:25; 13:55; Mark 3:31-35). This implies she had other children.

Jesus had half-brothers and half-sisters. At the beginning of His ministry, His brothers and sisters were indifferent to, or critical of, Jesus. However, after the crucifixion, they became active Christians and leaders of the early church (Acts 1:14). James became the leader of the Christian church in Jerusalem and wrote the New Testament letter that bears his name. Another half-brother, Jude, wrote the epistle of Jude in the New Testament.

*"And it came to pass, as he spake these things, a certain woman of the company lifted up her voice, and said unto him, Blessed is the womb that bare thee, and the paps which thou hast sucked. But he said, Yea rather, blessed are they that hear the word of God, and keep it."*

**Luke 11:27-28**

One day, an unnamed woman listened to Jesus as He taught. The woman yelled out, *"Blessed is the womb that bare thee, and the paps which thou hast sucked"* (Luke 11:27), When this woman yelled to the Lord about his mother, He had the perfect opportunity to venerate Mary. But there is no indication here from Jesus that Mary was to be venerated.

*"And the angel came in unto her, and said, Hail, thou that art highly favoured, the Lord is with thee: blessed art thou among women."*

**Luke 1:28**

71

The word, "hail" means "hello." It does not mean "to worship." The angel is greeting Mary by saying hello. "Highly favored" literally means "full of grace." The same Greek word is used of Christians by the Apostle Paul in Ephesians 1:6 where it is translated "accepted." In other words, the angel is saying, "Hello Mary, you have been favored by God." Mary is not to be worshiped because she has grace that she can give to others. She is a recipient, not a dispenser of divine grace.

*"And she spake out with a loud voice, and said, Blessed art thou among women, and blessed is the fruit of thy womb."*

**Luke 1:42**

When Mary went to visit her cousin, Elisabeth greeted her by saying, "Blessed art thou among women." Elisabeth did not say, "You are blessed above women." She said, "You are blessed among women." She did not worship Mary.

Mary was not to be worshiped, but the Bible shows her to be an example for us to follow. She is a remarkable, admirable example of what God can do through an ordinary life completely surrendered to His keeping care and plan. When you read what the Bible says about Mary, you find a wonderful example of how to have a "Mary" Christmas.

Of all the women in the world, God chose Mary. Why? Why did God choose Mary? Why was this very young woman (she was only 14 to 17 years of age) given the honor of bearing the Son of God? What was so special about Mary?

## MARY WAS SPOTLESS
## BEFORE GOD

*"And in the sixth month the angel Gabriel was sent from God unto a city of Galilee, named Nazareth, To a virgin espoused to a man whose name was Joseph, of the house of David; and the virgin's name was Mary."*

**Luke 1:26-27**

Mary was spotless before God. She was sexually pure. The Bible says she was a virgin.

Today, many reject the doctrine of the virgin birth of Jesus Christ. Many believe it to be nothing but a "childish myth." Even many modern-day theologians say the virgin birth is a "nonessential legend."

However, if Jesus was not born of a virgin, but was the mere offspring of two human parents, then he was just a man – no different from any other human being, then His life had no special significance beyond being a great moral teacher. If Jesus was not born of a virgin, then His death had no meaning beyond the death of any other human being.

If Jesus entered the world through natural human reproduction, He would have simply been one more child in this fallen world. He would've been a reproduction of two human parents and would have inherited their sin nature.

If Jesus was not virgin born, He was not the Son of God. The death of the mere human being could not redeem humanity. It took a direct intervention of God, through Jesus entering this world through the virgin birth and then dying on the cross for the sins of the world. To deny the virgin birth is to deny the gospel. The Savior who died for our sins was none other than the Baby who was conceived by the Holy Spirit and born of a virgin.

Once a woman took her 16-year-old daughter to the doctor. "Okay, Mrs. Jones," the doctor asked, "What's the problem?" The mother said, "It's my daughter Darla. She keeps getting these cravings. She's putting on weight and is sick most mornings." The doctor gave Darla an examination. He then turned to her mother and said, "Well, I don't know how to tell you this, but your Darla is pregnant – about 4 months would be my guess." The mother was shocked and said, "Pregnant? She can't be, she has never ever been left alone with a man. Have you Darla?" Darla quickly said, "No mother! I've never even kissed a man!" The doctor walked over to the window and just stood there looking out. About five minutes of silence passed until finally the mother said, "Is there something wrong out there, doctor?" The doctor replied, "No, not really. It's just that the last time anything like this happened, a star appeared in the east and three wise men came over the hill. I'll be darned if I'm going to miss it this time!"

If you took biology in high school, you know it is physiologically impossible for a virgin to give birth. The only way it could happen is by a miracle from God. Modern biologists, scientists, and doctors argue for a virgin birth to be true, a Y chromosome had to have been created out of nothing in Mary's ovum, because she would not have possessed the genetic material to produce a male child. However, for the God Who created the universe, creating a Y chromosome is child's play.

The virgin birth is essential to the Christian faith for three reasons. First, it relates to the integrity of the Bible as God's word. The Bible says point-blank that Jesus was born of a virgin. If that's not true, then what can we believe in the Bible?

Second, the virgin birth relates to the integrity of Jesus as Messiah. For Jesus to be our Savior, three conditions had to be met. He had to be human. No angel could die for our sins. He had to be divine. A mere mortal could not bear the price that had to be paid for our sins. He had to be sinless. A sinner could not die for the sins of others. The virgin birth guaranteed the fulfillment of all three of these conditions – because He was born of Mary, He was human. Because He was conceived by the Holy Spirit, He was divine. Because He was born holy, without a sin nature, Jesus was qualified to serve as our Savior.

Third, the concept of the virgin birth was not some afterthought. It was prophesied thousands of years before Jesus was born. The very first messianic prophecy in the Bible is found in Genesis 3:15 where we are told that the Messiah would be born of the seed of a woman.

*And I will put enmity between thee and the woman, and between thy seed and her seed; it shall bruise thy head, and thou shalt bruise his heel.*

**Genesis 3:15**

The "seed of the woman" is a prophecy about a future descendent of Eve who will defeat the serpent and reverse the curse brought on by his deception. Most of the time, the Bible speaks of the seed of men, but in this case, it is the "seed of the woman." This prophecy clearly points to the future virgin birth of Christ – a birth in which the seed of a man is not involved.

According to this prophecy, the "seed of the woman" will receive a temporary wound from Satan (thou shalt bruise his heel). However, Satan will be completely crushed beneath the feet of the "seed of the woman."

Crucifixion victims would eventually die from suffocation. As their body gave out, the crucified person would push up with their feet to get a breath. This resulted in the person's heels scraping against the wood of the cross, thereby causing bruising. On the cross, Satan only bruised the heels of Jesus. Death could not defeat Him. One day, He will return and crush Satan's head.

*"Therefore the Lord himself shall give you a sign; Behold, a virgin shall conceive, and bear a son, and shall call his name Immanuel."*

**Isaiah 7:14**

Over 700 years before Jesus was born, Isaiah prophesied the Messiah would be born of a virgin. Further, Isaiah said He would be God in flesh. He would be "Immanuel" which means "God with us."

Larry King, the former CNN talk show host, was once asked whom he would most want to interview if he could choose anyone from all of history. He said, "Jesus Christ." The questioner said, "And what would you like to ask him?" King replied, "I would like to ask him if he was indeed virgin-born. The answer to that question would define history for me."

We already have the answer to that question. The virgin birth of Jesus Christ defined history.

Mary was sexually pure when Jesus was conceived by the Holy Spirit in her womb. In our world today, God still wants to use people who are pure. The purity God is looking for goes beyond the physical. God is looking for people who are pure in their hearts and mind.

The Lord Jesus Christ forgives us when we fail, but you should strive in your life to be pure – to be spotless before God. It takes work and effort with all the trash that is out there on the internet, phones, television, and whatever. You must flee from these things. God will only take up and use clean vessels. Mary was spotless before God. So in turn, God could use her.

## MARY WAS SURE OF GOD

*"Then said Mary unto the angel, How shall this be, seeing I know not a man?"*

**Luke 1:34**

Mary was sure of God. She was filled with faith. She knew the Old Testament - about the miraculous births of Isaac, Samson, and Samuel. However, there had never been a birth without a human father. The angel tells her that she is going to have a child even though she is still a virgin. Mary believed the angel. She believed it was going to happen. She just needed an explanation of how it was going to happen.

Jewish betrothals were as binding as marriages, but couples did not come together as man and wife until the betrothal period was over. Mary and Joseph were still in the betrothal period, yet Gabriel said she would become pregnant. Mary knew she was still a virgin. Her question was a simple one: How?

When the angel explained everything to her, she responded in faith. She believed the impossible – that she, a virgin, would conceive and have a child.

Think about what must have been going through Mary's mind. To be a Jewish woman and be pregnant before marriage meant she would be an outcast. She would be scorned. There would be public humiliation for herself and her family.

Mary risked losing Joseph. She was getting ready to spend the rest of her life with the man she loves. Now, she will have to tell him she is pregnant. He will know he is not the father. Undoubtedly, he will call off the wedding. Mary risked losing the happy dream every girl has of a beautiful wedding. She risked losing her husband.

Mary also knew her child would be labeled illegitimate. Apparently, this label followed the Lord for the rest of his life. There is an interesting detail in Mark 6:3. Jesus returned to his own country. On the Sabbath day, he taught in the synagogue. The people were amazed at his teaching and said, "*Is not this the carpenter, the son of Mary, the brother of James, and Joses, and of Juda, and Simon? and are not his sisters here with us? And they were offended at him.*" Notice they call Jesus the "*son of Mary.*" The normal Jewish practice would be to identify a son by his father's (Joseph's) name. They did not do that here because they remembered the rumors of Jesus' illegitimate birth. A man was called the son of his mother if his father was unknown. They were insulting Jesus.

None-the-less, Mary set aside all her own desires and dreams to obey God. She knew God, and she was sure He would work out all the details. She was willing to put her life in His hands.

The Old Testament opens with a woman making a tragic choice. In the Garden of Eden, Eve made the choice to distrust God. The result was the entire world was plunged into sin and chaos.

The New Testament opens with another woman making a wonderful choice. Mary made the choice to trust God. The result was the entire world received a Savior.

## MARY WAS SCHOOLED
## IN THE WORD OF GOD

*"And Mary said, My soul doth magnify the Lord, And my spirit hath rejoiced in God my Saviour. For he hath regarded the low estate of his handmaiden: for, behold, from henceforth all generations shall call me blessed. For he that is mighty hath done to me great things; and holy is his name. And his mercy is on them that fear him from generation to generation. He hath shewed strength with his arm; he hath scattered the proud in the imagination of their hearts. He hath put down the mighty from their seats, and exalted them of low degree. He hath filled the*

*hungry with good things; and the rich he hath sent empty away. He hath helped his servant Israel, in remembrance of his mercy; As he spake to our fathers, to Abraham, and to his seed for ever."*

**Luke 1:46-55**

Mary was schooled in the Word of God. She knew the Scriptures. Luke 1:46-55 records what theologians call the "Magnificant" or the "Song of Mary." Mary's praise to God is full of biblical images, phrases, and references. There are 27 allusions to the Old Testament books of Genesis, Deuteronomy, 1 Samuel, 2 Samuel, Job, Psalms, Isaiah, Ezekiel, Micah, Habakkuk, and Zephaniah. Mary had absorbed and internalized the word of God.

Most 15-year-olds today cannot even remember John 3:16. Mary's example shows us that young people can have a heart for the things of God. God is not asking you to be a theologian. Just read the Bible, internalize it, and apply it to your life.

## MARY WAS SUBMISSIVE TO GOD

*"And Mary said, Behold the handmaid of the Lord; be it unto me according to thy word. And the angel departed from her."*

**Luke 1:38**

Mary refers to herself as the *"handmaid of the Lord."* In other words, she is saying she is a common slave for God. She humbly submitted to God's will. Someone once said, "God made everything that exists out of nothing and as long as we are nothing, God can make something out of us." That is how Mary sees herself.

Mary did not object. She did not say, "Wait a minute Gabriel. You've got the wrong person." She was open and receptive to what God wanted to do in her life.

A recently licensed pilot was flying his private plane on a cloudy day. He was not very experienced in instrument landing. When the control tower wanted to bring him in, he began to get panicky. Then a stern voice came over the radio, "You just obey instructions, we'll take care of the obstructions."

God is looking for people He can use to do the impossible. If you will just obey His instructions, He will take care of the obstructions. If you want to grow in your faith, you must be willing to let God use you and take you where you have never been.

What does God want to do in your life?

Are you ready for it?

Is your heart open to the possibility of what God is trying to do in and through you?

# Chapter 5
# THE CARPENTER

"He was her man and she was his wife
And late one winter night
He knelt by her as she gave birth
But it wasn't his child, it wasn't his child"

Skip Ewing

## Joseph

*"Is not this the carpenter's son? is not his mother called Mary? and his brethren, James, and Joses, and Simon, and Judas?"*

**Matthew 13:55**

One day a little boy was at the barber shop getting his haircut while his father was waiting for him. The boy was fascinated by the barbershop's Christmas tree, which was adorned with lights and decorations. He turned to his father and asked, "Daddy, why can't we have a Christmas tree in our house?"

His father said, "Jewish houses don't have Christmas trees."

The little boy thought for a moment and then with a frown on his face replied, "Daddy, why did we have to buy a Jewish house?"

Joseph was from a Jewish house. He was from the house and lineage of David. God chose Joseph to be the earthly parent of our Lord. He was the man who would teach, discipline, guide, and train Jesus as He grew. He would be a friend and even teach Him his trade as a carpenter. Israel's Messiah was raised by a Jewish carpenter in a Jewish house.

*"The book of the generation of Jesus Christ, the son of David, the son of Abraham."*

**Matthew 1:1**

*"And Jacob begat Joseph the husband of Mary, of whom was born Jesus, who is called Christ."*

**Matthew 1:16**

*"And Jesus himself began to be about thirty years of age, being (as was supposed) the son of Joseph, which was the son of Heli."*

**Luke 3:23**

It has become very popular today to trace your genealogy. Ancestry.com is a website that boasts an annual profit of over $200 million. However, there are a few things in the Bible that are less meaningful to the modern reader than the genealogies. People who read the Bible do mental gymnastics when they come to the lists of these biblical names. No author today would think to begin a book or story with such a list. One of the primary tenants of creative writing is to capture the attention of your reader in the first paragraph. A genealogical table would cause most modern readers to turn away. However, for the ancients and particularly for the Jews, this was an eye-catching way to begin a book. Genealogies in ancient times not only established identity, but also showed status.

The New Testament provides two genealogies of Jesus. One in Matthew, the other in Luke. Matthew's genealogy is the genealogy of Joseph. Matthew traces Jesus' lineage through David's son, Solomon. Luke is the genealogy of Mary. Luke traces Jesus' lineage through David's son, Nathan. Joseph was the legal father of Jesus, but not the literal or biological father. On the other hand, Jesus is a physical descendent of Mary. Her genealogy established the right of Jesus to David's throne. Mary's genealogy was the legal genealogy which presented Jesus' right to rule over the House of David.

Matthew opens his account of the Christmas story with a statement that would be familiar to his Jewish audience – *"The book of the generation of Jesus Christ."* Literally, it could be translated – "This is the genesis of Jesus Christ." Matthew begins with Abraham and works his way down to Joseph. Luke begins with Joseph and works his way back to Adam who was created by God. If you combine Luke's genealogy with John 1:3, *"All things were made by him; and without him was not any thing made that was made."* – in the beginning Jesus created Adam and Eve.

America has become obsessed with celebrities. We live in a day when we idolize the latest Hollywood actor, or football player, or singer. We are a country that is preoccupied with stars. Our infatuation with celebrities has even gotten into the church. There are certain names in Christian circles that carry a lot of weight – names like Franklin Graham, Robert Jeffers, Charles Stanley, Tony Evans, and David Jeremiah. Their names are famous, and their opinions are important to us. We seek them out, even in areas where they might not have much expertise, because they are famous.

There are famous people in the Bible too – names like Moses, David, Paul, and even Mary. Their faith makes them larger than life. God used them to change the world.

You and I will most likely never part the Red Sea. We may never kill a giant with a slingshot. We may never literally see the hand of God work miracles. Most of us are just every day, ordinary people. So, that is why I believe it is important to look at the life of somebody like Joseph.

Truthfully, we know very little about Joseph. He is not mentioned very often in the Bible. Mary is the one who takes up most of the passages that have to do with Christ's birth. The Bible never records one word spoken by Joseph. He is more of a background figure.

However, Joseph was the man God trusted enough to take care of His very own Son. He was the man God chose to trust with as a helpless baby, a vulnerable child. God trusted this man with one of the greatest responsibilities in the history of the world.

So, we need to look at a life like Joseph's and learn what we can, because Joseph is somebody like us. Joseph is a member of the supporting cast in the movie. He is one of the faces in the background.

## JOSEPH WAS A
## BENEVOLENT MAN

*"Now the birth of Jesus Christ was on this wise: When as his mother Mary was espoused to Joseph, before they came together, she was found with child of the Holy Ghost. Then Joseph her husband, being a just man, and not willing to make her a public example, was minded to put her away privily."*

**Matthew 1:18-19**

87

Joseph was "*espoused*" to Mary. The engagement was usually arranged by the parents while the children were very young. When they were of age, they were betrothed. The betrothal usually lasted for one year. During that time the girl lived with her parents, but the couple was looked upon as being husband and wife. During this stage of betrothal, unfaithfulness was regarded the same as adultery. After the betrothal year was over, the wedding ceremony was held, and the bride went to live with her husband. It was during the betrothal period, that Mary was found to be with child.

What a shock that must have been to Joseph. How would you or I have reacted had we heard something like, "Joseph, your girlfriend is pregnant, and it isn't yours!" That sounds like something from *The Jerry Springer Show*. It is hard to imagine how he felt when he first discovered Mary was pregnant. He knew that he wasn't responsible for the pregnancy. It must have looked as if Mary had been unfaithful to him.

The Jewish Law said if a betrothed woman became pregnant by a man that wasn't her husband, she was to be killed (Deuteronomy 22). In our contemporary society, it is difficult for us to understand, but adultery was a serious crime in the ancient world. In Egypt, it was punished by cutting off the nose of the adulteress; in Persia, the nose and ears were cut off; in Israel, the punishment was death by stoning. In Joseph's eyes, Mary had committed a crime worthy of death.

No, for Joseph to marry Mary now would be unthinkable: she is defiled; she is under God's judgment. A righteous man could have nothing to do with her. At the very least, she should be publicly disgraced and let the people decide how to deal with her.

I imagine in Joseph's mind his world has fallen apart. His plans for the future were in tatters. What is he going to do about it? As a righteous man he could not marry her; as a just man he ought to hand her over to be judged. However, in his inner struggle, as he prayed to God about it, and wrestled internally, the quality that prevailed was not justice, but mercy. Joseph was a man of mercy. He did not want to expose Mary to public disgrace. So, he had in mind to divorce her quietly.

Divorce proceedings among the Jews of the first century could be handled privately. A man could bring charges against his wife quietly and give her a written statement of divorce. The woman had no legal recourse but to accept this decree. Joseph had no intention of making a public spectacle of Mary. He planned to show mercy to Mary by handling the matter quietly.

When Napoleon was the Emperor of France, a woman once approached him to ask for a pardon for her son. Napoleon replied that the young man had committed the crime twice and justice demanded death.

"But I don't ask for justice," the mother explained. "I plead for mercy."

"But your son does not deserve mercy," Napoleon replied.

"Sir," the woman cried, "It would not be mercy if he deserved it, and mercy is all I ask for."

"Well, then," the emperor said, "I will have mercy." So, he spared the woman's son.

Justice would demand that each one of us bust open the gates of hell and sizzle like a sausage for all the sins we have committed. But God has granted us mercy through Jesus Christ. When God picked a man to trust to take care of His Son, He found Joseph – a benevolent man – a man who understood mercy.

## JOSEPH WAS A
## BELIEVING MAN

*"But while he thought on these things, behold, the angel of the LORD appeared unto him in a dream, saying, Joseph, thou son of David, fear not to take unto thee Mary thy wife: for that which is conceived in her is of the Holy Ghost."*

**Matthew 1:20**

*"Then Joseph being raised from sleep did as the angel of the Lord had bidden him, and took unto him his wife."*

**Matthew 1:24**

God sent an angel to explain the situation to Joseph. When he woke up, he did what God told him to do. None of Joseph's friends knew the explanation. All the people publicly did not know. None-the-less, despite this public confusion and suspicion he obeyed the Lord and did what God said.

If you read on in the other Gospels, you learn a little more about Joseph. In Chapter 2 of the Gospel of Luke, we read that Joseph had gone back to the home of his family, the town of Bethlehem. He went there because of the census and he couldn't provide a place for his wife to have a baby. Think about that. Bethlehem is the home of his family. Joseph had relatives in Bethlehem. Why doesn't his family take them in? Maybe they looked down on Joseph in disgrace because of all that was happening with Mary. However, no matter what family thought, Joseph believed and was obedient to God.

## JOSEPH WAS A
## BACKGROUND MAN

Joseph was the carpenter of the town of Nazareth. He was not just a carpenter, but 'the" carpenter. Later, in Matthew Chapter 13, Jesus was referred to as "'*the' carpenter's son.*" A little town like Nazareth could not afford more than one carpenter. So, here he was. Joseph, the town's carpenter – a tradesman.

Joseph was involved with the day to day life of the people of Nazareth. The carpenter was not shut away. He would have been out on the main street. His shop would have been open to the dusty road allowing for people to wander in and out with their things to be repaired and their orders to be built. Joseph was intimately connected with the day to day life of the people of Nazareth. Joseph was a man with callouses on his hands and sweat on his brow who was involved in the day to day ministry of the people in his time.

One of the greatest lessons I have learned from the life of Joseph is there might be invisible Christians, but there are never unimportant ones. As a Pastor, I am the out-front guy. I am the man the public sees. However, there are at least thirty to forty people that are involved in putting together our weekly church service.

In every organization there are the visible and the invisible. In a church you've got your ministry, you've got your song leaders, you've got your teachers, and you've got a pastor. However, there is a much larger group of invisible people – those who bring food, those who clean the buildings, those who mow the grass, those who make bulletins, those who work behind the scenes.

Joseph was that sort of person too. Not a splashy person, but someone God spoke to and someone that God used. God uses regular people with regular lives. There is never anyone unimportant to God and there is never anyone unimportant to God's plans.

Your life may seem routine right now. You might be doing the same thing today that you were doing yesterday and that's okay. Raising kids, working hard, studying, whatever it is, it's okay because God is in that routine. He is building in you the kind of character that you will need when those bigger moments come.

God worked in Joseph and when Joseph arrives on the scene in Matthew 1, he was already a man of character. That character was built across a period of years. So, it's okay if life is routine. Someday, your big moment will come. The challenge is to obey when God calls.

Like Joseph, whether you are in a routine or whether you are at that big moment, be the kind of person who hears what the Lord says and obey.

That was the kind of man God chose to trust Himself with as a helpless baby. Joseph was a man who was merciful, obedient, and worked in the background to do whatever it took to make sure God's will was done.

God trusted Himself to Joseph, and He will trust Himself to you too. The very first Christmas, God trusted Himself to Joseph. Wouldn't it be wonderful this Christmas if God were able to trust you with more of Himself?

Have you opened your heart to Christ?

What happened to Joseph? The Bible doesn't tell us much more about the man. Forty days after Jesus' birth, Joseph and Mary presented the infant Christ to the Lord at the temple (Luke 2:22-39). At His dedication, an old prophet named Simeon said only to Mary, *"Yea, a sword shall pierce through thy own soul also"* (Luke 2:35a). Simeon spoke only to Mary which suggests the sorrows of Calvary would affect Mary, but not Joseph.

When Jesus was 12-years-old, Joseph and Mary took Him to Jerusalem for the Passover (Luke 2:41-51). Nothing more is heard of Joseph afterward. At no time does he appear again during the three-year public ministry of Jesus. Most Bible scholars believe he died in the meantime.

Joseph, like you and I, was not a witness to the miracles. He never saw the blind receive sight, the leper cleansed, or the dead raised. He never saw Jesus on an old rugged cross dying as a suffering Savior. He never saw an empty tomb. Still, he had enough faith to believe.

Do you?

# Chapter 6
# THE CARAVAN

"Christmas is based on an exchange of gifts:
the gift of God to man –
His Son; and the gift of man to God –
when we first give ourselves to Him."

Vance Havner

## Wise Men

*"I shall see him, but not now: I shall behold him, but not
nigh: there shall come a Star out of Jacob, and a Sceptre
shall rise out of Israel, and shall smite the corners of
Moab, and destroy all the children of Sheth."*

**Numbers 24:17**

I am the man at my house. In fact, I was talking to some
men at church the other night and I was telling them

about a serious argument between my wife, Amanda, and I. The argument ended when Amanda came crawling to me on her hands and knees. That's the truth. Amanda came crawling to me on her hands and knees.

One of the men was impressed and he said, "What did she say when she came crawling to you on her hands and knees." "She said, 'Come out from under that bed and fight like a man, you coward...'"

Here's the truth: One of these days, everyone in the world will be on their hands and knees. One day, every person will kneel before the Lord Jesus Christ.

One of the most brilliant men of the 17<sup>th</sup> Century was the English Poet, Charles Lamb. One time, Charles Lamb and a group of intellectuals were talking. One of them asked what they would do if some of the gifted men of the past were to enter the room. Charles Lamb said, "If Shakespeare were to enter, we would rise to our feet in admiration, but if Jesus Christ were to enter, we would kneel and worship in adoration."

Charles Lamb was correct. The only proper response to the person of Jesus Christ is to fall and worship Him. We don't rise to shake His hand. We fall to kiss His feet.

All of history is headed to the feet of Jesus Christ. One of these days, the Lord Jesus Christ will stand once again on this earth. When He returns, every knee shall bow, and every tongue shall confess that Jesus Christ is

Lord. In the meantime, we should live our lives in the present at the feet of Jesus.

When Christ was born, He had some mysterious visitors known as the magi or wise men. We don't know much about them. However, we do know the wise men had the proper response. They came and fell at the feet of Jesus.

The wise men believed they could learn the truth by looking at the stars. So, God sent them the most incredible star they had ever seen. They followed the star and it brought them to the Truth. If you seek God with all your heart, you will find Him.

*"Now when Jesus was born in Bethlehem of Judaea in the days of Herod the king, behold, there came wise men from the east to Jerusalem."*

**Matthew 2:1**

When Jesus was born, wise men came from the east. The word "wise" means *magi*. Many believe they were kings, but the Bible never calls them kings. They are magi not kings. The only three kings in the Christmas story are Caesar, Herod, and the King of Kings.

"Magi" was a title given to people of the eastern countries who held positions of authority. Magi comes from the root word magician. These men studied black magic, the occult, astrology, as well as astronomy.

Belteshazzar was the most famous of all the magi. You know him better as the Prophet Daniel. Belteshazzar was the Babylonian name given to Daniel (Daniel 1:7). In 605 BC, King Nebuchadnezzar captured Jerusalem and took captives with him back to Babylon. Among the captives was Daniel, who was made a eunuch and added to the wise men of Babylon. Later, Daniel gained great fame as a wise man and interpreter of dreams.

Throughout the book in the Bible that bears his name, Daniel made predictions about the coming Messiah including his prophecy of the 70 weeks of years (Daniel 9:24-27). This remarkable prophecy established the general time period of the Messiah's coming by indicating it would be 483 years after a Persian ruler issued a decree to rebuild Jerusalem. The wise men had probably been counting down the years since the Jews had been sent back from Babylon to rebuild Jerusalem, and they knew the general time the Messiah would be born.

Daniel also referred to night visions. So, the wise men were focused on the constellations in the night sky as they looked for an indication of the birth of Messiah. They were looking to the heavens for a sign.

The wise men also had access to the writings of Moses (the Torah). From these writings, they may have come across the messianic prophecy of Balaam that a star shall come forth from Jacob (Numbers 24:17). The wise men were astrologers. They sought to understand human events by reading the constellations. They compared the skies to prophetic literature, including the Jewish Scriptures which spoke of the "King of the Jews" whose coming would be heralded by a star.

The wise men were from the east. During Old Testament times, the Jews had contact with both the Babylonians and the Persians. A large colony of Jews remained in Babylon even after the Jewish exile ended. Those Jews often spoke of a coming Jewish King that would rule the world. Therefore, the wise men were interested in the promise of this coming King and when they saw the star, they were curious enough to follow it.

But think about this – the wise men, whoever they were and however many there were, put their entire lives on hold to come see the Christ child. Babylon, which is in modern day Iraq, was located 800-miles from Jerusalem. The methods of travel were primitive. It took weeks if not months to make this trip. They were completely and totally immersed in the goal of seeing the Christ child for themselves.

## THE WISE MEN
## PURSUED FAITH

*"Saying, Where is he that is born King of the Jews? for we have seen his star in the east, and are come to worship him."*

**Matthew 2:2**

The wise men pursued faith. They had enough faith to follow where the star led them. Faith comes by hearing and hearing by the Word of God (Romans 10:17). The wise men knew the prophecies of Daniel. They knew the Word of God. The long arm of God's love had reached out and was tapping at their heart and soul. The Holy Spirit was leading them to Jesus. The wise men were drawn to Jesus Christ by the Holy Ghost.

We don't know how many wise men there were. At Christmas, we sing the song, *We Three Kings* because they brought three gifts, but we don't know how many there were. Being guys, there may have been nine or ten of them and they all went in on the gifts. Who knows?

Some sources say there were indeed three wise men and their names were Melchior, Balthasar, and Gaspar. They were also believed to have come from three different nations (Babylonia, Persia, and India). However, there is no evidence other than tradition to support these claims. You would be just as well off in believing the wise men were named Larry, Moe, and Curly and they came from Walla Walla, Chattanooga, and Cincinnati.

My wife once told me, "If the three wise men had been three wise women, they would have asked for directions, arrived on time, helped deliver the Baby, cleaned the stable, and made a casserole." That may be true, but the fact remains, we don't know if there were 3 or 300 wise men.

The wise men traveled in a large caravan – a large camel train. Many servants, cooks, and guards would have traveled with them. Herod would have not noticed three men on three camels. This was a big caravan with many people. Such a large caravan would have attracted much attention.

The wise men were Gentiles. They did not belong to the commonwealth of Israel. The Jews, who should have been looking for Him, did not seek Him, but these Gentiles traveled a great distance to find Jesus. The wise men journeyed over 800 miles to worship Jesus. I can't get people to drive three blocks to come to church and worship Jesus, but the wise men came a long way.

How far are you willing to go to come to Jesus? If you are reading this and you are not a Christian, you may be thinking the distance is too far between you and God. Perhaps the Spirit of God is tugging at your heart right now, but you believe you are too far from God.

There is an old story about an atheist who died. Before he died, he had his will changed and he left his farm to the devil. He was a bitter old man and had no family or friends. So, he left his farm to the devil.

The court had to decide about the old man's farm. After a time of deliberation, the judge handed down the following decision. "It is decided that the best way to carry out the wish of the deceased is to allow the farm to grow weeds, let the soil erode, and let the house and the barn rot. In my opinion, the best way to leave something to the devil is to do nothing."

If you put off getting saved, you will end up having willed your soul to the devil. There is no distance that is too far between you and God.

Reach out to Him in faith.

## THE WISE MEN
## PERCEIVED NO FAITH

*"When Herod the king had heard these things, he was troubled, and all Jerusalem with him. And when he had gathered all the chief priests and scribes of the people together, he demanded of them where Christ should be born."*

**Matthew 2:3-4**

When the wise men arrived in Jerusalem, they perceived no faith. King Herod was certainly not a person of faith. Sadly, neither were the priests and the scribes. The priests and the scribes were the religious rulers of the day. They were the reverends and the doctors. They had D.Min., PH.D., DDT, TNT, BA, BO – they had all kinds of titles out by their name. These men were experts in the Old Testament.

*"And they said unto him, In Bethlehem of Judaea."*

**Matthew 2:5a**

The priests and the scribes knew the Word of God, but they didn't know the God of the Word. However, they were familiar enough with the Bible to know about a prophecy in Micah Chapter 5, that said the Messiah would be born in Bethlehem, five miles south of Jerusalem.

*"For thus it is written by the prophet, And thou Bethlehem, in the land of Juda, art not the least among the princes of Juda: for out of thee shall come a Governor, that shall rule my people Israel."*

**Matthew 2:5b-6**

King Herod was an Edomite – a descendent of Esau. He was a false king. Herod had not been born king of the Jews. He had seized the throne by intrigue murder and power. Nothing disturbed him more than the fear that someone with a rightful claim would take the kingdom from him. During his later years nearly all of Herod's energies were directed against those who might be trying to steal his throne from him. The last thing Herod wanted was for a Jewish king to take his place. So, he was troubled when the wise men told him the King of the Jews was born and all of Jerusalem was troubled with him.

We have a saying at our house, "If Momma ain't happy, there ain't nobody happy." In those days in Jerusalem, "If Herod ain't happy, there ain't nobody happy."

103

When King Herod was troubled so was everyone else. In fits of rage, Herod had executed so many people that no one was sure whose head might be next. Therefore, when the people of Jerusalem heard Herod was troubled, they became troubled also.

Herod and all of Jerusalem were troubled, but they were not saved. They knew where the Savior was to be born. They had head knowledge, but they had no heart belief. It is possible to have Jesus Christ in your head and not have Him in your heart. It is possible to have all of the information, but to never experience regeneration. It is possible to have a religious affiliation and not have a religious conversion. It is possible to have your name on a church roll and not have your name in the Lamb's Book of Life. It is possible to have walked down an aisle in a church and never had Jesus walk into your heart.

These people had the very word of God in their hand that told them where the Messiah would be born, but they missed it. It's not enough to have it in your head, you must have it in your heart. You must come to Christ in repentance and faith and trust Him and Him alone to be your Savior.

At home, we have a jar of honey sitting on the kitchen counter. We often put honey in our tea. So, we have a jar of honey sitting on the counter by the stove.

Your mind can know honey is sweet because someone told you it is sweet. You can know honey is sweet because you have read books about it. However, if you haven't tasted it, then you know with your head, but not with your heart. When you taste it, you experience it for yourself. When you know it in a full way, you can know it in your heart.

When it comes to the Gospel, you need to learn in your head what Jesus has done for you, but more importantly, you need to learn it in your heart. It needs to become real to you, personally. Taste and see that the Lord is good (Psalm 34:8)

*"Then Herod, when he had privily called the wise men, enquired of them diligently what time the star appeared. And he sent them to Bethlehem, and said, Go and search diligently for the young child; and when ye have found him, bring me word again, that I may come and worship him also."*

**Matthew 2:7-8**

*"When they had heard the king, they departed; and, lo, the star, which they saw in the east, went before them, till it came and stood over where the young child was. When they saw the star, they rejoiced with exceeding great joy."*

**Matthew 2:9-10**

When God created the universe, He created the sun, moon, and the stars for "signs, and for seasons, and for days, and years" (Genesis 1:14). We are later told that the Jews "require a sign" (1 Corinthians 1:22). God created the heavenly bodies for signs. Before the foundation of the world, God put the galaxy in motion to point to the birth of Christ. God could have moved the planets, the stars, the entire creation to point to Christ's birth, but this was no ordinary star.

There are many theories about this star. Some say it was a comet with the tail pointing the way to Bethlehem. Some say it was an alignment of the planets Saturn and Jupiter. Some say it was a nova, or supernova – an explosion in deep space. Some say it was a meteor, or meteor shower. Some even argue that the star of Bethlehem was an unidentified flying object (UFO).

While most cannot agree on what the star was, everyone seems to agree on one thing: over 2000 years ago, something incredible happened in the heavens. Whatever it was, it was no ordinary star. Ordinary stars don't move. Ordinary stars don't appear, disappear, and then reappear. The star "went before" the wise men. It directed them to the village – to the very place where the Christ child was. It stopped over the area and pointed to the infant King.

This star was supernatural. It was the supernatural Shekinah glory of God.

The renowned messianic Jewish scholar, Alfred Edersheim (1825-1889), put forth another solution to the mystery of the star. He pointed out that the Greek word translated "star" really means "radiance." The "star" could therefore have been what the Jews called the

"Shekinah." The Shekinah glory was a physical manifestation of the glory of God in the form of supernatural radiance.

The Jews experienced the Shekinah in the wilderness of Sinai for 40 years when they were led by a pillar of cloud during the day, and a pillar of fire by night. (Exodus 13:21-22) When the radiant cloud moved, they moved. When the cloud stopped, they stopped and camped. (Numbers 9:15-23).

Later, the Shekinah resided in the holy of holies after the temple of Solomon was built (2 Chronicles 7:1-3). The prophet Ezekiel described how the Shekinah departed from the temple in stages before God allowed the temple to be destroyed by the Babylonians. (Ezekiel 9:3; Ezekiel 10:18-19; Ezekiel 11:23).

Considering the radiant and maneuverable qualities of the Shekinah that are demonstrated in the Scriptures, it seems the star which the wise men saw was really the Shekinah glory of God.

The star stopped right over where Jesus was located. The wise men went inside and worshiped Him. They believed with all their heart that this was the Son of God.

## THE WISE MEN
## POSSESSED FAITH

*"And when they were come into the house, they saw the young child with Mary his mother, and fell down, and worshipped him: and when they had opened their treasures, they presented unto him gifts; gold, and frankincense and myrrh."*

**Matthew 2:11**

The wise men possessed faith. Remember, they were Gentiles. They were not raised in believing homes, but they had faith. They believed in Jesus even though they had never seen Him. That's faith. Then when they found Him, they believed, and they worshiped Him. However, faith is not believing when you see. Faith is believing when you don't see. Faith is not believing because I see it is so. Faith is believing because God says it's so.

The wise men believed even though they were surrounded by unbelievers and hypocrites. Herod and his bunch were not interested in finding Christ except to kill Him. They sure didn't want to worship Him. The lesson for us is – don't let hypocrites rob you of your salvation.

Somebody once asked me, "Do you know there are hypocrites in the church?" Duh! Sure, I know there are hypocrites in the church. That is nothing new. Jesus had a church of 12 and one of them was a total dud. He was a hypocrite. I pray that hypocrites come to church every Sunday. They might get saved.

The wise men did not let the hypocrisy of Herod and his bunch keep them from coming to Jesus. The Holy Spirit brought the wise men right passed the hypocrisy and brought them straight to Jesus Christ.

The Holy Ghost won't bring you to Brigham Young. the Pope of Rome, Buddha, Allah, or James Collins. The Holy Spirit of God will take you to Jesus Christ for salvation. Only Jesus Christ can save your soul.

When you look at a nativity scene, you usually see the wise men. Hollywood and Hallmark have added them to the birth. The truth is, the wise men were not present at the birth of Jesus Christ. Scholars debate when they showed up, but all agree there is a time gap between several weeks and up to two years.

The wise men came *"into the house"* to worship Jesus. The word Matthew uses for house is always used of a permanent dwelling. Some time had passed because Joseph, Mary, and Jesus had moved from the barn to a house.

When the wise men came into the house, they *"saw the young child."* Some time had passed because Jesus was not referred to as a baby, but as a young child.

After they worshiped Him, the wise men gave gifts to Jesus. From these three gifts came the tradition of exchanging gifts at Christmas.

Many years ago, I gave my wife, Amanda, an engagement ring for Christmas. We had been dating for quite a while and one day I asked her, "Sweetie, what do you want for Christmas this year?" She said, "Now that I have you in my life, I don't want anything. You don't have to get me anything for Christmas." So, I didn't…I didn't know back then, when a woman says, "Don't get me anything," that means you had better get her something.

That Christmas, Amanda's parents invited me to their house. I was sitting in the living room with Amanda's Dad. She was in the kitchen with her Mom. I didn't know it at the time, but in the kitchen, Amanda was saying, "I can't believe that jerk didn't get me anything for Christmas. I can't believe I thought about marrying him!"

After everybody opened their gifts, I reached in my pocket and handed Amanda an engagement ring. She started crying. Her Dad started crying. Amanda cried tears that said, "I get to spend the rest of my life with the man I love." Her Dad cried tears that said, "I'm stuck with this idiot for a son-in-law for the rest of my life."

In a sense, it could be said that Amanda got me for Christmas.

Christmas gifts can be very special, but what gift do you bring to Jesus? It is still a custom in some parts of the world when you visit royalty, to bring a gift to the king. The wise men looked upon him as royalty, and as such they offered him their gifts.

The wise men brought Jesus four very appropriate gifts. I bet, you just went back and read that line again. You are right, I did say, "Four." The wise men gave Jesus four gifts.

First, they gave Him gold. Gold is a gift for a king. Since gold was looked upon as the king of metals, it was a gift suited for a king. So, the gift of gold was symbolic of the kingship of the Lord Jesus Christ. By giving Him gold, they said that He is a King.

Second, the wise men gave Him frankincense. Frankincense is the gift for deity. It was a resin that was collected from a tree that was at least 10-years-old. The resin was collected by hand. It was used to make an incense that was used in the temple rituals of sacrifice. The pungent fragrance of frankincense was thought to be pleasing to God. The odor of this spice filled the house of worship. By giving Him frankincense, they said He is our High Priest.

Third, they gave Him myrrh. Myrrh was also a resin. It was used as a painkilling drug. When Jesus was hanging on the cross, the soldiers offered Him sour wine mixed with myrrh, but He refused it. Myrrh was also used for embalming and anointing the body of a dead person. When Jesus was taken down from the cross for burial, Joseph of Arimathea and Nicodemus covered His body with spices – one of which was myrrh. Therefore, the gift bore witness to the fact that Jesus came to die for the sins of the world. By giving Him myrrh, they said that He was a dying Savior, who would shed His blood for the sins of the world.

Fourth, they gave Him themselves. They fell and worshipped Him. When they fell at the feet of Jesus, they said, "I give you my mind. I give you my motives. I give you my family. I give you my finances. I give you my heart. I give you my mind. I give you my soul. I give you my failures. I give you my dreams. I give you my all."

That's the greatest thing you could give Jesus.

This Christmas give Him you.

In 1988, Anissa Ayala was sixteen years-old when she was diagnosed with a rare form of Leukemia. The doctors said that if she did not receive a bone marrow transplant after chemotherapy and radiation treatment she would die. Neither her parents nor her brother were a match, and they could not find a donor anywhere else. Her parents, both in their forties, conceived another child and hoped the baby's bone marrow would be compatible with Anissa's.

After the baby was born it was determined this new baby was a compatible donor. When Marissa Ayala was fourteen months-old they took some of her marrow and gave it to Anissa. Anissa made a full recovery from the Leukemia. Today, both sisters lead healthy lives.

In a very real sense Marissa was born to save her sister's life. She says, "Without me being a perfect match for my sister, she would not be here."

Jesus was born into this world for the purpose of saving you. He is the one and only Savior that can save all those who put their faith and trust in Him.

Salvation is a gift. It is a gift given to you. By accepting this gift, you give a gift. You give yourself to Jesus. Are you ready to give Jesus His Christmas present? Do you believe that Jesus is the Son of God? Are you willing to turn from your old life of sin? Are you willing to let God transform you into a new creation?

Will you give yourself to Jesus?

*"And when they were departed, behold, the angel of the Lord appeareth to Joseph in a dream, saying, Arise, and take the young child and his mother, and flee into Egypt, and be thou there until I bring thee word: for Herod will seek the young child to destroy him. When he arose, he took the young child and his mother by night, and departed into Egypt: And was there until the death of Herod: that it might be fulfilled which was spoken of the Lord by the prophet, saying, Out of Egypt have I called my son."*

**Matthew 2:13-15**

God warned Joseph in a dream that Herod wanted to murder Jesus. As soon as he woke up, he took Mary and Jesus and fled down to Egypt. If they averaged 20 miles per day along the coastal route, Joseph, Mary, and the Child Jesus would have reached Egypt in about 10 days.

Six hundred years earlier, the Babylonians conquered Jerusalem. Many Jews fled to Egypt (Jeremiah 42-44). Many did not return to Israel at the end of the Babylonian captivity. There are several ancient historical documents that reveal Mary had family in Egypt, and they lived with her family during their time there. Joseph, Mary, and Jesus stayed in Egypt until Herod died.

Over the course of his life, Herod married 10 wives. He had many sons who all schemed to succeed him. Herod was so jealous of his favorite wife that on two occasions he ordered her to be killed if he failed to return from a trip. Eventually, he killed her anyway, as well as her grandfather, her mother, his brother-in-law, and three of his sons, not to mention numerous subjects. During a swimming party at Jericho, Herod drowned the high priest who happened to be another of his brother-in-laws.

Herod wrote to Rome asking for permission to execute one of his two sons for treason. This prompted his friend Caesar Augustus to say, "I'd rather be Herod's pig than his son."

Toward the end of his life, Herod began to worry no one would mourn his death. So, he issued orders from his deathbed that leaders from all parts of Judea were to be locked inside the great hippodrome at Jericho. When he died, archers were ordered to murder the thousands in cold blood, so there would be mourning associated with his death.

In the spring of 4 BC, Herod contracted a terrible disease that affected his digestive system, inflamed his abdomen, and blocked his breathing. After a last fevered convulsion, he died. His final plans – both of them – failed. The Jewish leaders who were jammed inside the hippodrome were not murdered but released. And the Baby who was supposed to die in Bethlehem was instead being carried in the arms of His mother as they sought refuge in Egypt.

*"Then Herod, when he saw that he was mocked of the wise men, was exceeding wroth, and sent forth, and slew all the children that were in Bethlehem, and in all the coasts thereof, from two years old and under, according to the time which he had diligently inquired of the wise men."*

**Matthew 2:16**

There is a famous children's story called, *How the Grinch Stole Christmas*. It was originally a huge best-selling book by Dr. Seuss. It was later made into a classic cartoon, a live action film, and more recently an animated major motion picture.

The Grinch is the story of a strange creature that hates Christmas. He hates Christmas so much that he tries to keep Christmas from coming. Herod wanted to do the same thing. Herod hated Christmas so much that he tried to stop it from happening in the first place. Herod wanted to eliminate the Christ child, so he murdered the children in Bethlehem.

Can you imagine the scene of mothers frantically trying to hush their crying babies so they would not be discovered only to see them snatched out of their arms by Herod's soldiers, thrown to the floor, and run through with swords? When we think about Christmas, we think of the little Baby in Bethlehem's manger. Sadly, there is another story attached to the Christmas story – the story of all the children who were killed by that blood thirsty Herod.

Near Christmas in 2012, a 20-year-old masked gunman dressed in black massacred 12 little girls, 8 little boys, and 6 women at Sandy Hook Elementary School in Newtown, Connecticut. There had only been one homicide in 10 years in this small community located about 60 miles northeast of New York City. The tragedy was devastating for the community especially for the parents of the 20 children and the families of the six adults. People asked, "How does this happen?" "How does this happen at Christmas?" "How could someone execute a six-year-old child?"

The first Christmas massacre was when the wise men sought to find the King of the Jews and the wicked King Herod sought to exterminate his rival by having all the boys under the age of two murdered in Bethlehem. It is estimated that the population of Bethlehem was between 500 and 600 people. Probably about the same number of children were murdered by King Herod as were murdered in 2012 at Newtown, Connecticut.

"Evil visited this community today," Connecticut Governor Dan Malloy said of the Newtown Christmas massacre. Something as wicked and evil as the murder of little children reminds us that not only is Jesus the reason for the season, but sin is also the reason for the season. The reason Jesus was born was so He could go to the cross and die for our sins.

Several years ago, there was a young man from a wealthy family who was about to graduate from high school. It was a custom in their affluent community for parents to give their graduating children a new car. The boy's dad spent weeks visiting one dealership after another, and the week before graduation they found the perfect car. The boy was certain it would be in the driveway on graduation night.

However, on the night of his graduation, his father handed him a small package wrapped in colorful paper. The father told his son the package contained the most valuable gift that the father could think to give him for his graduation. Thinking the box held the keys to the car, the son opened it, but instead of keys he found a Bible. The son was so angry that he threw the Bible down and stormed out of the house. He and his father never saw each other again.

Several years later, the news of the father's death finally brought the son home again. Following the funeral, he was sitting alone one evening. He had the task of going through his father's possessions. As he looked through everything he would inherit, he found the Bible he had thrown down years before. Overwhelmed by grief, he brushed away the dust and cracked it open for the first time. When he did, a cashier's check dated the day of his high school graduation fell into his lap in the exact amount of the car they had chosen together. The gift had been there all along, and if he had just opened his Bible, he would have found it.

Within the pages of the Holy Bible, you will find God's promise of satisfaction, salvation, and serenity for you. In the Bible, you will find God's gift for you all wrapped up in the person of Jesus Christ.

What are you going to do with God's gift?

Your response to God's gift depends on where you are at this point. Right now, you are in one of three places on your spiritual journey. You are either saved, lost, or out of touch with God.

If you are saved, you are already in a relationship with Jesus Christ. You have surrendered your life to Him. Jesus Christ is your Savior and Lord. I want to encourage you to celebrate with all your heart God's touch upon you this Christmas.

If you are lost, you have not yet unwrapped the gift of love He has for you. You've never opened the box of grace or received the gift of eternal life that God wants to give to you. Today can be the greatest day of your life. You can make that decision today and accept Jesus into your heart.

If you are out of touch with God, you once knew Christ, but for whatever reason you have drifted away from Him. You're not walking with Him like you used to. He used to be your close companion, but now you hardly acknowledge His presence anymore. I just want to let you know that God is calling you to come back home this Christmas. What better time than now to get reacquainted with Jesus and experience all over again the touch of God?

There's an old bumper sticker that says, "Wise Men still seek Him." That has never been truer than it is today. Surrender your life to Christ.

It will truly be the wisest choice you've ever made.

# Chapter 7
# THE CHRIST

"Do I want to see Christ back in 'Christmas'?
I'd rather see Christ back in Christians!"

Tom Holladay

## Baby Jesus

*"Now all this was done, that it might be fulfilled which
was spoken of the Lord by the prophet, saying, Behold, a
virgin shall be with child, and shall bring forth a son, and
they shall call his name Emmanuel, which being interpreted is, God with us."*

**Matthew 1:22-23**

Once upon a time, there was a great and marvelous
king who had an enormous kingdom. He was tremendously wealthy and had great authority. One day, the
king was out on his horse, and he was surveying all his
fields, and he saw a very common, peasant girl out

working and laboring in his vineyards. She had dirt all over her hands, sweat all over her brow, and she was wearing a dress that was tattered and threadbare. She appeared to be a very common, working-class kind of girl.

When the king saw her, he was instantly taken. It was love at first sight. He thought she was beautiful. There was something about her that attracted him. He wanted very much to marry her and spend the rest of his life with her. The king started to inquire about her. He discovered that she was poor in finances, but very rich in character. Everyone who knew her said she was wonderful.

The king knew if he went to her and said, "I'm the king, would you like to marry me," that if she said, "Yes," he would continually wonder whether she loved him because she truly loved him, or if she loved him because he was the king.

The king came up with a plan. He decided he would put on commoners' clothes. He decided to go undercover as a poor man. He took a job working in the vineyard right alongside the woman. He put his hands in the dirt and sowed seeds with her and reaped harvests with her. Each day and all day, he went to work and labored alongside his love. They talked throughout the day getting to know each other.

Over time, she fell in love with him. She adored him. She believed in all her heart that he was poor, simple, and common, but she loved him like that. One day he proposed marriage, and she accepted. However, he still didn't tell her he was the king.

He told her to put on a beautiful dress, and on a certain day, he would come and pick her up to take her to the wedding. He told her not worry about it because he would set up the wedding. He told her that he would surprise her.

So, she went home with her family and friends and waited. One day, an army of chariots, soldiers, banners, and musicians – thousands upon thousands showed up. They picked up this poor country girl from her little rural town, and they carried her into the city. They carried her right through the gates into the palace with trumpets blaring. Seated on the throne, she saw the king, and recognized him as the man who was going to be her husband.

She walked up to the king. He explained to her, "I wanted you to love me not because I was the king. I wanted you to love me simply for the sake of loving me. Only then, could I show you that I was the king, and I could know your love for me would always be true."

God did the same thing for us. God came in an unexpected way. He came in a humble, simple, regular, normal way, as a regular man, from a regular town, with a regular mom, and a regular dad, who lived a regular life. God came in this very simple way in the person of Jesus Christ. It was a way we never would have expected. The world didn't recognize him, and the Jews rejected him. They looked and said, "No, we are waiting for a king.

You're no king." Jesus said, "Well, I am a king, and if you love me, I will take you to the palace. But you have to love Me first."

When we think of the coming of the Lord Jesus Christ into the world, we do well to consider the fact that His coming was foretold in the Old Testament.

*"Therefore the Lord himself shall give you a sign; Behold, a virgin shall conceive, and bear a son, and shall call his name Immanuel."*

**Isaiah 7:14**

One day, Elmer and his brother Earl were walking down the street. They were talking as they went along, and Earl wasn't paying attention. He stepped off the curb and right into the flow of traffic. The driver of the car tried to stop, but unfortunately, he hit Earl.

This was in the days before cell phones. So, Elmer ran over to a pay-phone and called an ambulance. When the dispatcher answered, Elmer said, "Get an ambulance here quick. My brother was hit by a car. He is bleeding from his ears and nose and I think both of his legs are broken." The operator said, "What is your location, sir?" Elmer said, "On Acacia Street." The operator said, "How do you spell that sir?"

There was a silent pause. After a minute, the operator heard heavy breathing. Then she heard someone screaming in agony. She yelled into the phone, "Are you there, sir?" But there was no answer. She could still hear the heavy breathing and the screaming. That went on for another couple of minutes. The operator screamed, "Sir, are you there? Please answer me. Can you still hear me?" Finally, Elmer's voice came back on the line. He said, "Yes, I am still here. Sorry about that. I couldn't spell Acacia, so I drug him around to Oak Street."

That was a story with an unexpected twist. Seven hundred and fifty years before the birth of Jesus Christ, the Prophet Isaiah gave a prophecy with an unexpected twist. Whoever heard of a virgin conceiving and having a child? Yet 750 years before the birth of the Lord Jesus Christ, a promise was given that a virgin would have a child and the child would be called Immanuel.

In Bible times, parents would give their children names to symbolize certain events. For example, the name Moses means "drawn out" because they drew him out of the water. Names were also given to reflect a special mission God had for their life, or else it would reflect the hopes and dreams their parents had for them.

My daughter was named Abbigail because it means "father's joy." Amanda and I named her that hoping it would describe her character and spirit – it does. My son was named Timothy because it means "honoring God." We named him that hoping he lives a life that honors the Lord. My youngest son was named John which means "God is gracious." John got his name because he was a gracious gift from God.

My name, James Collins, means "Goofy Red-neck." I am still not sure what my parents had in mind when they named me...

However, when God gave a name, it was a way of revelation. God would often give a name that revealed truth. 750 years after this prophecy was given, there was a carpenter from Nazareth, a small town in Northern Israel. The carpenter was Joseph, and he was in a state of emotional distress and confusion.

Joseph was betrothed to a woman named Mary. He loved her desperately and looked forward to their life together. A betrothal was more binding than a modern-day engagement. It could only be dissolved by a decree of divorce. If someone was unfaithful during the betrothal, that was grounds for a divorce. The person who had been wronged could publicly humiliate and put away the unfaithful person. In addition, the person who had been wronged had the right to have the unfaithful person stoned to death.

Joseph had been told by Mary that she was going to have a baby. He knew Mary's Baby wasn't his child. The only explanation he could come up with was she had been unfaithful. However, he loved her so much that even though he could put her away publicly or even have her killed, he decided he would put her away quietly. Even though he was hurt, Joseph did not want to hurt the woman he loved.

*"But while he thought on these things, behold, the angel of the* LORD *appeared unto him in a dream, saying, Joseph, thou son of David, fear not to take unto thee Mary thy wife: for that which is conceived in her is of the Holy Ghost."*

**Matthew 1:20**

While Joseph thought on these things, the angel of the Lord appeared to him in a dream and said, "Don't put her away. Go through with the marriage because the Baby in her womb is there through the process of a miracle. The Holy Spirit visited the womb of Mary and conceived in her the Son of God."

*"And she shall bring forth a son, and thou shalt call his name* JESUS: *for he shall save his people from their sins."*

**Matthew 1:21**

Remember names were important in the Bible. The name God chose for His Son was a name that reflected God's nature and His character as it was revealed in human form. The angel told Joseph the Son to be born to Mary was to be called "Jesus."

Being a righteous Jew, Joseph would have been reminded of a verse of Old Testament Scripture by the angel's words. He would have been reminded of Psalm 118:14 which reads, *"The* LORD *is my strength and song, and is become my salvation."* The Hebrew word for salvation is *yeshua*. God will become salvation. God will become *yeshua*.

From the Hebrew word *yeshua* comes the name Yeshua (Joshua). The Greek translation for the name Yeshua is *Iesous*. The English translation for the Greek name Iesous is Jesus. Yeshua is the Hebrew name of Jesus.

God will become Jesus.

The Lord Jesus Christ had another name, too, but it wasn't one given to Him because the name "Jesus" was unsatisfactory. It was given to Him because of the added significance it would carry.

*"Now all this was done, that it might be fulfilled which was spoken of the Lord by the prophet, saying, Behold, a virgin shall be with child, and shall bring forth a son, and they shall call his name Emmanuel, which being interpreted is, God with us."*

**Matthew 1:22-23**

Seven-hundred-fifty-years after Isaiah predicted, *"Behold a virgin shall conceive and bear a son, and shall call his name Immanuel,"* the angel quoted Isaiah, and then added *"which being interpreted is, God with us."* That is the revelation. That is what God wants us to know: God, the Almighty of the universe, would come and be with us. Emmanuel, God with us.

A kindergarten teacher had gained a reputation of being able to communicate effectively with her four-year-old students. Some of the other teachers, hoping to learn the secret of her success, visited her in the classroom one day. There they found her on her knees in the middle of the room, busily involved in an activity with her class.

Later the visitors discussed her teaching methods with her and expressed some concern about her lack of dignity in getting on the floor with the children. "Well," she replied, "I don't know much about dignity, but I do know the only way to reach four-year-olds is to get down on your knees so you can talk to them face-to-face."

When God became Emmanuel, He got down on our level to talk to us face-to-face. God Almighty, the Creator of the universe, came to be with us. He is so big that He can't be measured. There is so much about Him that can't be understood. There is no way that you and I as sinners could climb our way up to Him. So, He came down to us.

God didn't come down to visit us in a palace. He didn't come down to visit us in a mansion. He didn't come down to visit us in a government headquarters. He didn't come down to visit us in the White House. God came down to be with us in a stable, in a little cave, where the animals were feeding because there was no room for Him in the inn. That is where God decided to come and meet with us and stay with us in the person of the Lord Jesus Christ.

The cry of the Baby in the Bethlehem manger was the cry of God. His little Baby hands were God's hands. The little face that Mary kissed was God's face. He was God with us.

## GOD WITH US
## SHOULD COMFORT US

The presence of God in our lives in Jesus Christ has certain practical implications. First of all, God with us should comfort us.

Life can be depressing. Several years ago, around Christmas, I preached a funeral for a man named Jon. In a fit of depression, Jon had taken his own life. On the day of his service, I stood before a flag draped coffin, and I tried to bring words of comfort to his grieving family. After the honor guard folded and presented the flag to Jon's widow, I said a prayer. When I started to pray, Jon's nine-year-old son, Kevin, began to wail. He cried and cried. When Kevin started crying, I did too. It broke my heart. I grieved for days for Jon's family and especially Kevin. Life can be depressing. This world is a mess and life is sometimes depressing.

Christmas can be a depressing time. Many people are depressed at Christmas because they are lonely. I believe people are lonely; not because their Mom died; not because their Dad died; not because their wife or husband left them – they are lonely because they really don't have

God. We were made to be with God and God to be with us.

God Who made the earth upon which we live and the galaxies upon which we gaze; God Who gave us breath in our lungs and gave us life; the God of all creation came to be with us. So, nobody needs to be lonely at Christmas or any time of year. God is with us. That brings me comfort.

For some people, Christmas can be depressing. Christmas can be lonely. I mean Christmas has become so commercial that somewhere along the line we have forgotten the whole meaning – God in the flesh came to be with us.

We get caught up in the presents, packages, parties, and preparations. We get so caught up we lose sight of Jesus in the whole mess and we get depressed and lonely.

Even some of the songs at Christmas can cause us to be depressed and lonely. When I was a kid, my Momma loved Elvis Presley. Every year at Christmas time, she would put on Elvis' Christmas Album. There is nothing that will make you feel more lonely, depressed, mournful, and sad than to hear Elvis sing *I'll Have A Blue Christmas* with the girls in the background going BLUUUUUUU. How depressing!

But you don't have to have a blue Christmas. God came to this earth. He walked around among us, and each day of your life, you will never walk alone if you are a believer because every step you take you will have a heavenly Companion. We should be comforted by God with us.

Many years ago, there was a man who had an unusual name. His name was Charlie Stink. As you can imagine, Charlie was the constant target of all kinds of jokes. Finally, his friends convinced him to go have his name legally changed, and he went to court. The next day one of his friends asked him what his new name was. He replied, "I changed my name to George Stink, but for the life of me, I can't see what difference it will make."

He missed the point.

Is your name "Charlie Stink?" Here's a recommendation for you: Don't change it to "George Stink." If you do, you will be missing the point of changing it at all.

Are you missing the point of Christmas? God with us says that God wants to know you, to be in relationship with you, to save you from your sin, and to be your Companion for all of eternity. Christmas is God with us and that should bring comfort.

## GOD WITH US
## SHOULD COMPEL US

Not only does God with us comfort us, it also compels us. If Jesus Christ is God, then you are compelled to obey Him. The only way to be fulfilled in this life is to study the Word of God and find out what He says and do it.

We live in a society that is at war with Christmas. The season seems to infuriate them. They're not angry at Santa Claus, the buying and selling, the endless variations of *White Christmas*, and fruitcakes. No. The real target of their anger is the story behind it all. Why? Because they know the story is true, not a myth. Because it is true, they understand the consequences.

There is no danger in not believing in Santa. However, there is considerable and eternal danger in not believing in Jesus. Christmas is a blessing for those of us who believe in Christ, but it is a threat to those who do not.

A few years ago, my wife, Amanda, and I were doing some Christmas shopping when I heard a cell phone ring. The ringing cell phone was in the purse of a woman standing next to me. She was by herself, and her phone continued to ring as she fumbled in her purse to find it. She was looking for her phone when she said, "Jesus Christ, leave me alone."

Those were her exact words. They were spoken to no one in particular, since she was alone, but I could hear frustration in her voice. It was as if her phone had been ringing a little too much recently and she was enjoying a few moments of being by herself – until her phone rang again.

"Jesus Christ, leave me alone."

I knew, and you know, that she did not intend to literally address Jesus Christ. She wasn't speaking to Jesus. She was using the name of the Lord as a cuss word. When that woman blasphemed the Lord, I thought to myself, "That is how the world feels about Christmas."

That woman was merely expressing in words what humanity has been saying for over 2000 years, "God, leave us alone. We don't want You interfering with us in our great big plans we have for living. We want to do what we want to do. We don't want You with us. God, leave us alone."

That's what the whole world was saying when God determined the time was right for His Son to be born. The whole world, including God's chosen people, the Jews, had been saying through their actions that they did not want God to tell them what to do.

We should not be surprised when the people of this world reject Christ. We should not be surprised when pagans act like pagans. We should not be surprised when lost people act like lost people. It should not surprise us that people who do not know Christ, say with their own lives, "Jesus Christ, leave me alone."

If you continue to reject Christ – if you continue to say, "Jesus Christ, leave me alone," – He will do just that. Once and for all you will get your way. God will leave you alone.

Forever.

Since Jesus is God with us, we are compelled to obey Him. Nike had a series of commercials that said, "Just do it." That is also true of the commandments we find in God's Word. We need to just do it.

"Cast all your cares on Him." Quit worrying and just do it.

"Turn the other cheek." Get over your bitterness. Just do it.

"Love your neighbor." Just do it.

"Confess Jesus before men." Just do it.

"Go the extra mile." Just do it.

"Thou shall not lie." Just do it.

"Forgive." Just do it.

"Love." Just do it.

Repent and believe the Gospel. Give your life to Christ and become part of a local church. Be baptized. Just do it!

Everybody wants Jesus as Savior. Nobody wants to go to hell. So, people want Jesus as Savior because they are looking for fire insurance – a get out of hell free card. It is true Jesus is Savior, but He is also Lord. He is Lord. He's the boss. God with us means He's the boss. It should compel us to obey Him. Just do it!

A truck pulled up to the border and a customs officer was suspicious. So, he ordered the driver out to search the vehicle. It was a complete thorough search. He searched the entire vehicle. He even pulled the door panels, bumpers, and wheel covers off and examined inside, but he did not find a single bit of contraband. Finally, the truck driver was waved through.

The next week, the same driver pulled to a stop at the border. The same officer was there. This time he was determined to find out what this guy was smuggling. Again, the officer searched, but again he found nothing illegal.

As time went on, full body searches, x-rays, and dogs were used, but every week the same man drove off with no illegal cargo ever to be discovered.

Finally, after many years, the officer was getting close to retirement. Here came the same driver. "I know you're a smuggler," the customs officer said. "Don't bother denying it. But I can't figure out what you have been smuggling all these years. I'm leaving now: I'm getting ready to retire. Please tell me what you have been smuggling."

"Trucks," the driver said.

The customs official totally missed the point.

Do you want Jesus as Savior, but not as Lord? If so, then you have missed the point. Christmas is God with us and that should compel us to obey Him.

## GOD WITH US
## SHOULD CAUTION US

God with us should caution us. Think about it: If Christ is God with us and you don't have Jesus Christ, then you don't have God. If you don't have God, then you don't have forgiveness. If you don't have God, then you don't have salvation. If you don't have God, then you don't have peace. If you don't have God, then you don't have heaven.

When Jesus Christ came for the first time in the history of man, people could actually treat God the way they always wanted to treat Him. When Jesus Christ came, they could actually get their hands on Him. So, what did they do? They spit in His face. They pulled out His beard. They beat the skin off His back. They put a crown of thorns on His head. They nailed Him to a cross. Jesus let them do all that. He allowed it to happen to pay your sin debt and to give you eternal life. Jesus did that for you.

This world is a mess. Most of the people in charge don't know their heads from a hole in the ground. It's like the inmates have taken over the asylum. They have taken Jesus Christ out of every aspect of life. They have taken down nativity scenes in public places. They have taken down crosses at Christmas displays. They have taken songs about Jesus off the radio and all they play are songs about Santa Claus. It's so bad, you can't even say "Merry Christmas" anymore.

Today, there are many well-known retailers who have attempted to take "Christ" out of "Christmas." These stores love it when the bells you hear at Christmas are from their cash registers. They are happy to take your money, but don't expect much mention of Christmas if you shop in those stores. They don't mention Christmas because a handful of atheists might be offended. However, they sure don't worry about offending Christians.

Those stores don't sell Christmas gifts. They sell "holiday" gifts. They don't close for Christmas. They close for a "holiday." They don't wish customers a "Merry Christmas." They wish them "happy holidays."

The world is a mess. The only hope we have is that God is with us. Jesus can come into a mess with a miracle. What the world needs is Jesus Christ the Son of God, and Satan knows it. That's why he wants to stop the very celebration of the birth of Christ. He wants to take every aspect of Jesus out of our lives.

But we don't have to stand for it. If you are saved, you have the presence of Christ with you wherever you go. You are a walking nativity scene. You have Jesus in you. The ACLU can't remove the nativity scene in your heart. Go to the courthouse, public schools, and government offices. Jesus is in you, He will be in the courthouse, public schools, and government offices.

Christians need to stop crying, whining, and retreating. God is with us! If Jesus is living in your heart, you need to remember, *"Greater is he that is in you, than he that is in the world"* (1 John 4:4). God is with us.

But you've got to believe. The Bible says that whoever shall call on the name of the Lord shall be saved and those who do not shall be lost. That should caution you.

Do you know Him today? Deep down in your heart, where it really counts, do you know Jesus' other name? Can you say His name is Emmanuel – God with me?

One December day in 1903 at Kitty Hawk, North Carolina, brothers Orville and Wilbur Wright, after numerous failures to fly in a heavier-than-air machine made amazing history. They did something no man had ever done before. They flew. Elated, they sent a telegram to their sister Katherine: "We have actually flown 852 feet. Will be home for Christmas."

Katherine was overjoyed. She wanted to share the news with everyone. She ran down to the local newspaper and pushed the telegram – the greatest news story of the century – into the hands of the editor. After reading it, he smiled and said, "Well, well, how nice. The boys will be home for Christmas." On December 19, the local newspaper placed the following headline on the sixth page: "Wright Brothers Home for Christmas."

The newspaper editor totally missed the point.

I am afraid we have missed the point, too. Do you go through the motions, perhaps even showing up for worship services every Sunday, or at least whenever it is convenient for you? Do you come in, pick up a bulletin, sing a few songs, listen politely to a sermon, visit with a few people on the way back to your car – but too often you never have an experience, a real encounter, with God?

This year, most people will miss the point of Christmas. Jesus Christ is present every Sunday, and every day, and every moment. The point of Christmas is God is with us. The blessing of Christmas and the message of Christmas is that God is with us.

On March 5, 1994, Deputy Sherriff Lloyd Prescott was teaching a class for police officers at the public library in Salt Lake City, Utah. Deputy Sherriff Prescott was not in uniform, he was in street clothes as he was teaching the police officers. Prescott heard a commotion and stepped out into the hallway just in time to see a man, later identified as Clifford Lynn Draper, herding 18 hostages at gunpoint into a room. The gunman did not notice him, so Deputy Sherriff Prescott just joined in with the eighteen hostages and became the 19th hostage. He allowed himself to be taken hostage.

The hostage taker began to talk about who he was going to kill first. He waved his gun in their faces. He made them get out sheets of paper to draw lots to determine which hostage that he would kill first. At that point, Deputy Sherriff Prescott drew his weapon and identified himself to the gunman. The gunman began to draw down on Deputy Sherriff Prescott, but the lawman was faster. Prescott killed the hostage taker in self-defense. All the hostages were released unharmed. The officer placed himself at great risk, but he wasn't thinking of himself, he was thinking about the danger the hostages were in.

At the first Christmas, God came down to earth dressed in street clothes. Like Lloyd Prescott, God dressed Himself as one of us and entered our world. He came down and He sort of blended in with the crowd. He came down here to be with all of those who were held hostage to Satan and sin. He joined us because we were held hostage to sin and in danger of spiritual death. On the cross, our Lord Jesus Christ, confronted the hostage taker and He defeated the devil. All the hostages in Jesus Christ are free now, free tomorrow, and free forever!

That's the meaning of Christmas. Jesus came to be with us, so He could die for us. So, He could live in us. So, He could forever be with us. That is what Christmas is all about!

What was the Baby's name?

Emmanuel.

His name is Emmanuel.

God with us.

# Chapter 8
# THE CONQUEROR

"Right now, Jesus is standing at the portals of heaven. Soon, He will turn the stars into a staircase and step into the sky just above the clouds. An angel will blow a trumpet that will break the sound barrier. The graves will shake, and Jesus will wake the dead. Then you and I that are living will blastoff through the air to meet the Lord in the sky. Jesus is coming again, and He's coming soon."

Dr. Fred Hambrick

## King Jesus

*"For the Lord himself shall descend from heaven with a shout, with the voice of the archangel, and with the trump of God: and the dead in Christ shall rise first: Then we*

*which are alive and remain shall be caught up together with them in the clouds, to meet the Lord in the air: and so shall we ever be with the Lord."*

**1 Thessalonians 4:16-17**

One year, Tom volunteered to help with Vacation Bible School at church. He was assigned to help with the preschool class. Tom wanted to be dramatic with the 4- and 5-year-old kids. So, he asked them, "Can any of you tell me what I've got to do to get to heaven?" Nobody answered. The kids just looked at him.

So, Tom said, "What if I sold my house and my car and gave all the money to the church? Would that get me to heaven?" The kids suddenly perked up and yelled, "No!"

Tom said, "What if I was a good person and obeyed all the laws of the land like a good citizen? Would that get me to Heaven?" All the little boys and girls screamed, "No!"

Tom said, "What if I loved my wife with all my heart? Would that get me to Heaven?" The children yelled out, "No!"

Finally, Tom said, "Well, will one of you tell me what I've got to do to get to Heaven?" A little five-year-old boy jumped up and said, "You've got to die, old man. You've got to die!"

For the most part, it is true that you must die to go to heaven, but not everybody is going to die. Some people will go to heaven without going through the graveyard. Some people will fly instead of die. Some people will be caught up to meet the Lord Jesus Christ in the rapture.

Throughout this book, I have looked at the first coming of Jesus – His first advent. His first advent was only part of the story. He is coming again. One day, Jesus will come again to rule the world – where every knee will bow, and every tongue will confess that Jesus Christ is Lord. That is His second advent.

*"And, behold, thou shalt conceive in thy womb, and bring forth a son, and shalt call his name JESUS. He shall be great, and shall be called the Son of the Highest: and the Lord God shall give unto him the throne of his father David: And he shall reign over the house of Jacob for ever; and of his kingdom there shall be no end."*
**Luke 1:31-33**

At Christ's first advent, the angel Gabriel appeared to Mary and made seven prophecies. Four of them related to the first coming of the Lord. All four have been fulfilled. Mary did conceive and bear a Son. His name was called Jesus. He was great. And He was called the Son of God.

The last three of the prophecies which Gabriel made to Mary have not been fulfilled. However, they will be when Jesus comes again. He will be given the throne of David. He will reign over the house of Jacob. And there will be no end to His kingdom.

All the prophecies of Christ's first advent were literally fulfilled. All the prophecies of Christ's second advent will also be literally fulfilled. He's coming again and He could return at any moment.

Are you ready?

*"He which testifieth these things saith, Surely I come quickly."*

**Revelation 22:20**

The word "surely" comes from a Greek word from which we get our English word "yes." Jesus is saying it's affirmative. You can count on it. Jesus is coming again.

There is much confusion and controversy when it comes to the Lord's second advent. It is beyond the scope of this book to try to sort out all the different end times viewpoints. Instead, I want to focus on what I believe.

I believe in the pretribulation rapture. I believe the rapture will happen before the seven-year period known as the tribulation. At the end of the tribulation, the Lord will return to rule the earth as King of Kings.

Many people disagree with the pretribulation rapture view because they say it teaches two second comings. However, the return of Jesus is not two second comings. There are two phases of the same event.

The first advent included multiple phases – His birth, life, ministry, death, resurrection, and ascension. When Jesus died, His spirit left His body. His spirit returned at His resurrection. This is not viewed as two advents, even though these two events were separated by three days.

Your life has had multiple phases. Your life began as an embryo. Then you developed into an infant. Now, you are a maturing adult. Each phase in your life was different and separated by time.

The first stage of the second advent, the rapture, will happen without warning and without signs. Christ will come suddenly to take His church to heaven. Seven years later, He will return with His church. He will defeat the enemies of God at the Battle of Armageddon and set up His Kingdom on earth.

The rapture is not a myth or a mistake. The rapture is not fiction, fable, or a fairytale. Jesus said in Revelation Chapter 22, "Count on it. I am going to come again." Then He adds this, "I am going to come quickly."

I have been preaching that Jesus is coming at any moment for years, but I have never believed more than I do right now. When I look at the world today and I see the signs of the times, I believe the brass section in Heaven's Orchestra is warming up. I believe the wedding hall is being decorated in Heaven for the Marriage Supper of the Lamb. I believe Jesus could come for the church any minute now. I believe the rapture could occur at any moment.

I don't know about you, but I've got my bags packed. I have accepted the invitation. I'm just waiting for my ride.

## THE RAPTURE
## IS IMMINENT

*"He which testifieth these things saith, Surely I come quickly."*

**Revelation 22:20**

Quickly means "very soon." His return is imminent. Imminent means it is ready to happen.

I grew up with my cousin Bubba. One day, when we were both about 8-years-old, we were acting up in church. Poppa leaned over and said to Bubba, "If you don't want what my boy is going to get when he gets home, you'll settle down." Then Poppa pointed his finger at me and said, "Boy, you know better than to cut up in church. I promise, you're going to get it when you get home."

Suddenly, my legs began to shake. My teeth began to chatter. I began to get all nervous and upset because I knew what "it" was. I had had "it" in a variety of ways. I had "it" with a paddle. I had "it" with a flyswatter. I had "it" with a switch. I had "it" with a belt.

The belt was Poppa's preferred way of administering "it." He had an old belt that was hung on a nail on the wall under a copy of that old hymn, *I Need Thee Every Hour* because he used "it" on me regularly.

Now please don't tell everyone I said to beat your kids and get me hooked up in a lawsuit. I didn't say that. I'm just telling you how I was raised. I was raised in a different time. I was raised by a generation that believed, *"He that spareth his rod hateth his son: but he that loveth him chasteneth him betimes"* (Proverbs 13:24).

In hindsight, I am glad Poppa loved me enough to discipline me. I wasn't beaten, or abused, but when I messed up, my backside was torn up. Today, I'm a better man because of "it."

Anyway, I was a nervous wreck. I sat there in church and I began to pray. I prayed, "Lord, let this be a long sermon today. Lord, please let the car break down on the way home."

Then I thought, well it doesn't matter how long "it" gets delayed. You are still going to get "it." My Poppa was a faithful promise keeper. Poppa promised me I was going to get "it." You could count on it that I was going to get "it."

However, as faithful a promise keeper as Poppa was, it does not compare to my Heavenly Father. He is the ultimate promise keeper. It doesn't matter if you've heard it all your life – Jesus said the rapture is coming. If Jesus said it, count on it.

# The Accuracy
# of Scripture

The rapture is imminent for two reasons. First, the rapture is imminent because of the accuracy of Scripture.

*"For I testify unto every man that heareth the words of the <u>prophecy</u> of this book, If any man shall add unto these things, God shall add unto him the plagues that are written in this book: And if any man shall take away from the words of the book of this <u>prophecy</u>, God shall take away his part out of the book of life, and out of the holy city, and from the things which are written in this book."*

**Revelation 22:18-19**

Prophecy means inspired predictions. Understand any idiot can make a prediction. There have been many over the years who have made predictions.

Journalist Junius Henri Browne predicted in 1893, "Law will be simplified over the next century. Lawyers will have diminished, and their fees will have been vastly curtailed." Wrong.

Computer scientist John von Neumann predicted in 1949, "It would appear we have reached the limits of what is possible to achieve with computer technology." Wrong.

Arthur Summerfield, the U.S. Postmaster General under President Eisenhower, predicted in 1959, "Before man reaches the moon, your mail will be delivered within hours from New York to Australia by guided missiles. We stand on the threshold of rocket mail." Wrong.

Computer expert Bob Metcalfe predicted in 1995, "The internet will go spectacularly supernova and in 1996 catastrophically collapse." Wrong.

Any idiot can make a prediction. I predict my wife will be mad at me before the day is over. I guarantee you that prediction will come true, but that does not make me a prophet. There's a difference between prediction and inspired prediction. Predictions come from a crystal ball. Inspired predictions come from the Creator. Predictions look to the stars. Inspired predictions look to the One Who hung the stars. There's a difference.

When I talk about prophecy, I'm talking about God declaring in advance something is going to happen in the future, and God's prophetic voice is correct 100% of the time. Only the Word of God contains fulfilled prophecies. The Bible predicted things before they happened and they actually happened. If the Bible was right before, it will be right about the prophecies that have yet to be fulfilled.

The prophecies fulfilled in the person of Jesus Christ are amazing. Three hundred Old Testament Prophecies were fulfilled in the life and death of Jesus Christ. Liberal theologians believe Jesus arranged it. They think He rigged it. Liberals say Jesus looked at the prophecies about the Messiah in the Old Testament and He rigged things to happen.

Micah predicted that He would be born in Bethlehem 700 years before He was born. How could Jesus have arranged where He was going to be born? Isaiah gave minute details about the life and death of Jesus 700 years before He was born. How could He have arranged to have His history written 700 years before He got here? Zechariah said a friend would betray Him for 30 pieces of silver 500 years before it happened. How could Jesus arrange Judas to betray Him and arrange for it to be for 30 pieces of silver?

David, predicted in the 22$^{nd}$ Psalm, thirty-three prophecies about the death of Christ. Psalm 22 predicts His hands and feet would be pierced. Psalm 22 predicts they would gamble for His clothes. Psalm 22 even quotes the words out of the mouth of Jesus 1000 years before He said them. Jesus didn't look back and quote David. David looked forward and quoted Jesus 1000 years before He got here. Jesus did not arrange His life to fulfill prophecy.

Also, Jesus did not accidentally fulfill prophecy. Mathematician, Peter W. Stoner, estimated the probability of Jesus fulfilling only eight Old Testament Messianic prophecies were 1 in $10^{17}$ or 1 in 100, 000, 000, 000, 000, 000. That's one in 100 quadrillion. Our minds cannot comprehend a number that big.

Stoner drove home the meaning of this number with this illustration. Imagine filling the state of Texas knee-deep in silver dollars. Include in this huge number one silver dollar with a black checkmark on it. Then turn a blindfolded person loose in this sea of silver dollars. The odds that the first coin he would pick up would be the one with the black checkmark are the same as eight prophecies being fulfilled accidentally in the life of Jesus.

The chance of a blind man finding a marked coin in a sea of coins in one try are the same as the prophets had for only eight prophecies accidentally being fulfilled in the life of Jesus. Which is no chance. Stoner only calculated eight of the over 300 prophecies. Figuring the odds of fulfilling all 300 Bible prophecies is astronomical. It is incalculable – unless the real author of these prophecies knew the future. The God Who created the universe out of nothing was in total control and knows the past, present AND future.

God predicted in minute detail events from the life of Jesus Christ, and God has predicted in minute detail events about when Jesus Christ will return for His church. Jesus is coming again. You can count on it.

## The Account
## of the Signs

Second, the rapture is imminent because of the account of the signs. In the 24th Chapter of the Gospel of Matthew, Jesus was gathered with His disciples at the Temple in Jerusalem. His disciples asked Him when will the end of this age come. Jesus tells His followers what the conditions will be like before He comes back to the planet.

Reading Matthew 24 is like picking up a newspaper. All the signs Jesus predicted are happening today. One could fill an entire book on the signs of Matthew Chapter 24. I just want to look at a couple.

### *War*

*"And ye shall hear of wars and rumours of wars."*

**Matthew 24:6a**

There has not been a war somewhere on this planet in only 60 of the last 500 years. The world has been in a constant state of war. America has been at war since September 11, 2001. My children have never lived in an America that has not been at war. Islam has declared war on the world. The President of Iran has made it his mission "to exterminate all Christians and Jews from off the face of the earth." Wars are tearing the world apart and will continue to do so until Jesus returns.

### *Natural Disasters*

*"...there shall be famines, and pestilences, and earthquakes, in divers places."*

**Matthew 24:7b**

Jesus said before He returns, there would be a rise in natural disasters. In the past ten years, there have been 3,852 natural disasters that have killed more than 780,000 people, affected more than 2 billion others, and cost a minimum of $960 billion dollars. The number of natural disasters in the world has tripled since the 1990s. In August of 2005, Hurricane Katrina totally wiped out a United States city. New Orleans was wiped out, not by wars or weapons, but by wind and water.

Jesus said before He returns there would be a rise in famines and diseases. Today we have West Nile, HIV, Zika, Ebola, H1N1, influenza, Middle East respiratory syndrome, severe acute respiratory syndrome, yellow fever, hantavirus, Nipah, Hendra, Marburg, and dengue. Every day, there seems to be another virus with a peculiar name lurking around the corner, poised to become the next global health emergency. Most of these viruses have no cure. Have you heard of the bird flu? I'm so worried about the bird flu, I haven't eaten at Kentucky Fried Chicken since it started...

These are signs of Christ's second coming, but there is not one sign that must be fulfilled before the rapture. There is a difference in the rapture and the second coming. At the rapture, He is coming in the clouds. At the second coming, He is coming through the clouds. At the rapture, He is flying alone. At the second coming, He is riding a horse. At the rapture, He is coming for His church. At the second coming, He is coming with His church. At the rapture, He is coming to take out. At the second coming, He is coming to take over – and He will rule forever as King of Kings and Lord of Lords.

The clear teaching of Scripture is the rapture must come before the second coming and these are second coming signs. They are happening right before our eyes. The trumpet of the Living God could sound at any moment.

Whenever possible, I like to eat at Cracker Barrel. The food at Cracker Barrel is so good that if you put one of those Country Dinner Plates on top of your head, your tongue would beat your brains out trying to get to it. The food at Cracker Barrel is delicious.

Whenever I go to eat at the Cracker Barrel, I enjoy shopping in the Cracker Barrel Store. Last June, I was in the Cracker Barrel Store and I noticed a shelf along the back wall that had Christmas items on it. It was June and Cracker Barrel had Christmas Stuff out!

A Cracker Barrel employee was standing by the shelf. I said, "Isn't it a little early for Christmas stuff?" She said, "Probably, but this is just a little shelf of stuff. We really don't start decorating until September." Then she said, "When I see all this Christmas stuff out, I start getting excited about Thanksgiving." She said, "My kids live all over the country. We don't see them at Christmas, but they take a whole week off at Thanksgiving. They all come home for Thanksgiving." She said, "Every time I see Christmas stuff up, I get all excited because Thanksgiving is going to come before Christmas."

The signs of the Christmas second coming are all around us, but the Thanksgiving rapture has got to come first.

On December 7, 1941, the Japanese attacked Pearl Harbor, thereby drawing America into World War II. Most people know what happened on December 7, 1941, but not very many people know what happened on December 9, 1941. On December 9, 1941, the United States Ambassadors to Japan, Italy, and Germany were called home. America was about to unleash the full force of its military on Japan, Italy, and Germany. So, we called all the Ambassadors home.

If you are a Christian, you are an ambassador for Christ (2 Corinthians 5:20). We are only in a temporary land. One of these days, the full fury of the wrath of God is going to be unleashed and poured out on this planet, but before it happens, Jesus will call His ambassadors home.

Are you ready?

## THE RAPTURE
## IS IMMEDIATE

The rapture is immediate. It will happen in an instant. If you believe the rapture could happen at any moment, it will change the way you live in every way.

*hew you a mystery; We shall not all sleep, but be changed, In a moment, in the twinkling of ie last trump: for the trumpet shall sound, and the ueuu ...hall be raised incorruptible, and we shall be changed."*

**1 Corinthians 15:51-52**

The rapture will happen in a moment. In the twinkling of an eye. A twinkling is faster than a "blinkling..." The eye is the fastest moving part of the human body. The eye blinks in 1/50<sup>th</sup> of a second. You are not even aware that you are blinking.

### Are You Saved?

The rapture will happen very quickly. In the twinkling of an eye, in a flash, you will be gone. So, you must be sure of two things. First, you must be saved.

Are you saved? If not, you are gambling with your eternal destiny. You believe you have plenty of time. You intend to get saved one day. One day, you plan to get right with God. Listen, you need to get saved when the Holy Spirit prompts you. That voice inside of you right now is the Holy Spirit telling you what you are reading is true. Jesus could come at any moment and you will be left behind. Do you know that you are saved?

## Are You Serving?

Second, you had better be sure you are serving. The Bible says, *"Therefore, my beloved brethren, be ye stedfast, unmoveable, always abounding in the work of the Lord, forasmuch as ye know that your labour is not in vain in the Lord"* (1 Corinthians 15:58). The word "therefore" is there because Paul just said the rapture could happen at any moment. Therefore, get busy doing whatever work God has given you to do.

Is there something you could be doing for God? There are hundreds of ways you could do something for God. You could take a meal to a sick friend. You could pray for someone. You could call and encourage someone going through a tough time. You could help with VBS. There are hundreds of ways you could do something for God. If you believe Jesus Christ could come at any moment, you should be doing something for Him.

## THE RAPTURE
## IS AN INTERRUPTION

The rapture will be an interruption. Jesus will return like a *"thief in the night"* (2 Peter 3:10). That is talking about His second coming. If people are going to be caught off guard by His second coming, how much more surprised will they be by the rapture. Jesus is not going to yell, "I'm coming tomorrow. Y'all get ready!" He's going to come like a thief in the night. People's lives will be interrupted.

One night a thief broke into a house he thought was deserted. As he walked through the darkened house with a flashlight he heard a voice from the kitchen that said, "Jesus is watching you." He stopped and said, "Who's there?" There was no answer so he thought he must have imagined it. But after he took a few more steps, the voice said again, "Jesus is watching you." He decided to walk toward the voice. Just before he entered the kitchen, he heard it again. "Jesus is watching you." He swung his flashlight up and saw a talking parrot in a cage. The parrot said, "Jesus is watching you." The thief flipped on the kitchen light and said, "Why you're just a dumb bird." Then he noticed a huge Doberman crouching under the cage. The parrot said, "Sic 'im, Jesus."

You talk about being interrupted by Jesus.

One day a businessman took his young son with him when he went to work. When they got to the building where he worked, the businessman told his son to stay by the door and soon he would return for him. However, the businessman got busy, the hours passed, and somehow, he forgot what he had said. He ended up going out a different door than the one he had entered. When he got home, his wife asked him about their son. He couldn't believe he had forgotten his son. Frantically, he hurried back to his building as fast as he could. The businessman found his son where he had left him. He was tired, cold, hungry and scared, but he was waiting just as he had been told to do. When he saw his father, he smiled and said, "I knew you would come. You said you would."

It's been 2000 years since the first advent. Believers wonder why Jesus hasn't come back yet. Some people say He has forgotten us. Some people say He made other plans. It's been a long time from our point of view, but He's only been gone for a couple of days from heaven's perspective. Jesus said He would come back - and He will. You can count on it.

You had better get ready or get left.

When he was four-years-old, my youngest son, John, discovered how to work the DVR. He would often record cartoons and watch them over and over. Just before Christmas, John recorded the Christmas cartoon special, *Grandma Got Run Over by a Reindeer*. He must have watched it a hundred times.

When January rolled around, we were taking down the Christmas decorations. John came in and turned the TV on and started watching *Grandma Got Run Over by a Reindeer*. I said, "John, you shouldn't watch that show anymore. Christmas is over." "No," John said. "Christmas isn't over. Christmas is coming."

Just as sure as He came the first time, Jesus is coming again.

Is He coming for you?

# Conclusion
# THE CHOICE

## Your Gift

*"For God so loved the world, that he gave his only begotten Son, that whosoever believeth in him should not perish, but have everlasting life."*

**John 3:16**

The word gospel literally means "good news." However, to understand the good news, you must start with the bad news. The Old Testament Law was given to Israel during the time of Moses (Deuteronomy 5:1). The Law is like a measuring stick, and sin is anything that falls short of "perfect" according to that standard. No human being could possibly follow it perfectly. We have all sinned (Romans 3:23), and the punishment for sin is death and separation from God in a place called hell. The Law established the fact that cleansing from sin can only happen through the shedding of blood (Hebrews 9:22).

## THE CRADLE

God sent his only Son into this world 2,000 years ago. He was not born in luxury or splendor, He was born in a stable and laid in a manger. The focus of this book was the Nativity story, but Jesus didn't stay in a manger.

## THE CROSS

Jesus grew up. He healed the sick, raised the dead, gave sight to the blind and fed the hungry. He said radical and awesome things that millions of people today still live their lives by. Jesus never owned an office, never wrote a book, never got a university degree, never owned a house; in fact, He never travelled more than 200 miles from the place of His birth. He did none of the things we associate with power and importance, but He was the most important person in history.

When Jesus was in His early thirties, He died on a cross. His death paid the price of our sin. His body was buried in a tomb, but He rose again from the dead. The grave is empty. Jesus is alive.

## THE CROWN

Jesus was born into this world, He walked this earth, because He loved each of us. Even if it was just for you, he would still have come to the earth. What a thought! That is how awesome God thinks you are, how special you are to him. He loves you more than words can say.

This Christmas, God offers you a gift. Not a gift you will lose interest in by tomorrow. He offers you Jesus. He offers you peace this world cannot offer. He offers you the unconditional love of the God who made you. He offers you a relationship. He offers you the assurance that you will go to heaven.

Quite simply... He offers you life.

Someday, soon, He is coming back again. When He returns, He will rule and reign as King of Kings and Lord of Lords.

## THE CHOICE

This Christmas, you have a choice. Don't just let the story of Christmas be a cute little story. Allow the wonder, the joy, and the mystery of Christmas to enter your life and change you. Christmas is about Christ – His cradle, His cross, His crown, and your choice.

One day a little boy was playing with a nativity set. He held up the figure of Baby Jesus. His mother asked, "What are you doing?" He replied, "Nothing. Just playing with Jesus."

Are you just playing with Jesus?

Where are you in your relationship with Him?

Do you know Him as Savior and Lord?

# HOW TO RECEIVE
# JESUS CHRIST

1. Admit your need (I am a sinner).
2. Be willing to turn from your sins (repent).
3. Believe that Jesus died for you and rose from the grave
4. Through prayer, invite Jesus Christ to come in and control your life through the Holy Spirit (receive Him as Lord and Savior).

## WHAT TO PRAY

Dear Lord Jesus,

I know that I am a sinner and I need Your forgiveness. I believe that You died for my sins. I want to turn from my sins. I now invite You to come into my heart and life. I want to trust and follow You as Lord and Savior.

In Jesus' Name. Amen.

# ABOUT THE AUTHOR

James Collins currently serves as Senior Pastor at First Southern Baptist Church in historic Fort Scott, Kansas. He has served in various pastoral positions in Kansas, Oklahoma, and California. Before accepting the position in Fort Scott, James was a chaplain in the United States Army and served in Operation Enduring Freedom, Operation Iraqi Freedom, Operation New Dawn, and Operation Inherent Resolve.

A life-long learner, James has four graduate degrees and is in the dissertation phase for the Doctor of Ministry Degree at Midwestern Baptist Theological Seminary in Kansas City, Missouri. He loves reading, especially books on Bible prophecy.

James is married to the love of his life, Amanda Collins. They have three incredible children, Abby, Timothy, and John. They live in Southeast Kansas where they are restoring a Victorian house.

You can find more information on his books and ministry at www.thepointis.net.

I would love to hear your story of how this book impacted your faith walk. If you write to me (james@thepointis.net), I will pray for you in your journey.

If you have given your life to Christ....
I wish you a Merry Christmas and a Happy New You.

James Collins

# BIBLIOGRAPHY

Boa, Kenneth and William Proctor. *The Return of the Star of Bethlehem*. Garden City, New York, 1980.

Cahn, Jonathan. *The Book of Mysteries*. Lake Mary, Florida: Charisma House Book Group, 2016.

Church, J.R. "The Place of Our Savior's Birth." *Prophecy In The News* December 2009: 3. Print.

Clarkson, Kevin. "Unto Us a Child is Born...A Son is Given." *Prophecy In The News* December 2016: 3-5. Print.

Cornuke, Robert. *Tradition: Exploring The Roots of Church Traditions*. Coeur d' Alene, Idaho: Koinonia House, 2018.

DeHaan, M.R. *The Birthday of the King*. Grand Rapids: Radio Bible Publishing, 1963.

Freeman, J.M. and J.H. Chadwick. *Manners & Customs of the Bible*. North Brunswick, New Jersey: Bridge-Logos Publishers, 1998.

Glaze, Bob. *Angels: A Historical & Prophetic Study*. Oklahoma City: Hearthstone Publishing, 1998.

Hutchings, Noah W. "Christ Was Conceived on Christmas Day." *Prophetic Observer* December 1995: 1-4. Print.

Jeremiah, David. *Why the Nativity?* Carol Stream, Illinois: Tyndale House Publishers, 2006.

Jones, Nathan E. "Was the Bethlehem Innkeeper a Schmuck?" *Lamplighter* November December 2015: 12. Print.

Keener, C.S. *The IVP Bible Background Commentary: New Testament.* Downers Grove, Illinois: InterVarsity Press, 1993.

Maier, Paul L. *First Christmas: The True and Unfamiliar Story.* New York: Harper & Row, 1971.

McGee, J. Vernon. *Through The Bible Volume IV.* Nashville: Thomas Nelson, 1983.

Mills, M.S. *The Life of Christ: A Study Guide to the Gospel Record.* Dallas: 3E Ministries, 1999.

Morris, Henry M. *The Genesis Record.* San Diego: Creation-Life Publishers, 1976.

Paschall, H. Franklin and Herschel Hobbs, eds. *The Teacher's Bible Commentary.* Nashville: Broadman Press, 1972.

Pfeiffer, Charles F. and Everett F. Harrison, eds. *The Wycliffe Bible Commentary.* Nashville: The Southwestern Company, 1968.

Reagan, David R. "The Miracle of the Incarnation." *Lamplighter* November December 2018: 2-3. Print.

Reagan, David R. "The Promises of Christmas." *Lamplighter* November December 2006: 2-3. Print.

Radmacher, E. D., R.B. Allen, and H.W. House, H. W. *Nelson's New Illustrated Bible Commentary.* Nashville: Thomas Nelson Publishers, 1999.

Schaeffer, Dan. *In Search Of...The Real Spirit of Christmas*. Grand Rapids: Discovery House Books, 2003.

Seevers, Boyd. *Hidden In Plain Sight*. Minneapolis: Bethany House Publishers, 2012.

Simmons, Billy E. *Be Born in Us Today*. Nashville: Broadman Press, 1982.

Spargimino, Larry. *Digging Deeper*. Oklahoma City: Bible Belt Publishing, 2008.

Stauffer, Douglas D. *One Book Stands Alone*. Millbrook, Alabama: McCowen Mills Publishers, 2001.

Stearman, Gary "The Christmas Prophecy of Bethlehem." *The Prophecy Watcher* December 2016: 4-9. Print.

Stoner, Peter. *Science Speaks*. Chicago: Moody Press, 1969.

Strobel, Lee. *The Case for Christmas*. Grand Rapids: Zondervan, 2005.

*The Holy Bible: King James Version*. (electronic ed. of the 1769 edition of the 1611 Authorized Version). Bellingham WA: Logos Research Systems, Inc., 1995.

Wiersbe, Warren W. *The Bible Exposition Commentary Volume 2*. Wheaton, IL: Victor Books, 1996.

Yancy, Phillip. *The Jesus I Never Knew*. Grand Rapids: Zondervan, 1995.

Youngblood, Ronald F., F.F. Bruce, and R. K. Harrison, eds., *Nelson's New Illustrated Bible Dictionary*. Nashville: Thomas Nelson Publishers, 1995.

# ALSO AVAILABLE

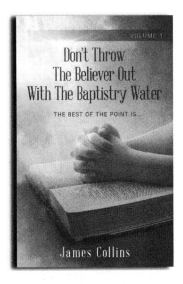

*Don't Throw The Believer Out With The Baptistry Water* is a collection of *The Point Is...*, the weekly newspaper column written by Pastor James Collins. Within these pages you will find the wit and wisdom of a country preacher. He is a natural-born storyteller with a talent for reducing everyday occurrences into messages that pack a spiritual punch. His stories have been called "modern-day parables."

"I loved this book. James is a natural story teller. One page I am laughing out loud, the next, I am wiping away the tears."

Pat Matthews, Louisiana

"This was an excellent book filled with wonderful life lessons for everyone. It was very easy to read, and I enjoyed it tremendously."

Edward Alford, Oklahoma

"This book is full of awesome, funny stories. I laughed and cried. Definitely a worthwhile read!"

Brian Williams, Kansas

Get your copy today at:
www.thepointis.net